True, Right, Better:

A Defense of the Christian Worldview

Dr. John M. Oakes

ILLUMINATION
PUBLISHERS

True, Right, Better: A Defense of the Christian Worldview
© 2023 by Dr. John M. Oakes

Printed in the United States of America. ISBN: 978-1-958723-94-4.

Cover and book interior design: Toney Mulhollan.

Illumination Publishers titles may be purchased in bulk for classroom instruction, business, fund-raising, or promotional use. For information please email paul.ipibooks@me.com

Illumination Publishers is committed to caring wisely for God's creation and uses recycled paper whenever possible.

John Oakes was a professor of chemistry in physics for 34 years at Grossmont College. He retired in 2018, and led a church in Bakersfield,

and now a new church planting in Merced, California. John became a Christian while attending graduate school in 1978. He earned a Ph.D. in chemical physics in 1984 from the University of Colorado. That same year he married his wife, Jan. They make their home in Merced, California. John also serves as president of the Apologetics Research Society. Some of his other books include: *The Christian Story, Volume I-4, Is There A God?, From Shadow to Reality, Reasons for Belief, Daniel: Prophet to the Nations, That You May Believe, Field Manual for Christian Apologetics* and *Golden Rule Membership.* For more about John's work and ministry, go to his website at www.EvidenceForChristianity.org.

Illumination Publishers International
www.ipibooks.com

CONTENTS

Dedication

I dedicate this work to my good friend and mentor Dr. Robert Kurka, formerly of Lincoln Christian University. He is the one who inspired me to go down this road. He challenged me personally to move from purely evidential apologetics to the importance of studying worldview in spreading the Christian gospel. Robert was not only an intellectual mentor, but his was one of the most truly Christian lives I have known. His life, his dedication to his students, to his family and to his church are exemplary. My only regret is that my friend did not live to see this dedication. When he was near death, I called to encourage him, but instead he encouraged me, saying, "I will see you soon." Thanks, Dr. Robert Kurka.

Introduction

Let us imagine the scene recorded in John chapter eleven. We are at Bethany, the home of Lazarus, Mary, and Martha. From the evidence of the New Testament, it appears that the three siblings are very close friends of Jesus—even as close as some of the apostles. Lazarus becomes deathly ill. Jesus has already publicly healed thousands from a wide range of illnesses—the blind, the deaf, the lame, lepers, and people with fevers, and he has even raised at least two people from the dead (Jairus' daughter, Luke 8:40–56 and the widow of Nain's son, Luke 7:11-17).

For this reason, Mary and Martha send friends to plead with Jesus to heal their brother. Given all the strangers he has healed, surely he will race to Bethany to save Lazarus from death. Shockingly, Jesus says that he is too busy right now to come. We have the inside information in the Gospel of John, allowing us to understand that Jesus knows exactly what he is doing here. He plans to raise Lazarus from the dead, thus giving glory to his Father. But let us think about this event from the vantage point of an unnamed participant at the scene who, like Mary and Martha, expects Jesus to come immediately. Why did Jesus not come to heal his friend?

Four days after Lazarus' death, Jesus finally arrives at Bethany on his way to Jerusalem, where he will be executed in just a few days. "Many Jews," perhaps hundreds, are gathered in Bethany to mourn the death of Lazarus. Mary and Martha are beside themselves with grief, to the point that Martha berates Jesus for not coming sooner. Jesus goes out to the tomb, where he encounters loud wailing and cries of anguish. Out of compassion, Jesus weeps for the bereaved. Then he stuns the crowd by demanding that the stone be removed from the cave where Lazarus' body has been laid. *"But Lord, by this time there is a bad odor, for he has been there four days"* (John 11:39). Despite this obvious fact, the authority of Jesus is sufficient for a group to go ahead and remove the stone. Then, Jesus loudly demands, *"Lazarus come out."* Nearly all in this crowd have seen multiple miracles performed by Jesus. Nevertheless, they are astounded when Lazarus walks out of the tomb with the strips of linen from his burial still on his body and his face.

Our interest in these events lies not in the story itself but in the two radically opposed reactions to this history-changing resurrection of Lazarus. I love the simplicity of John's description of one group. "Therefore, many of the Jews who had come to visit Mary, and had seen what Jesus did, believed in him" (John 11:45). Well, I suppose so! Not surprising! For these witnesses, their entire understanding of Judaism will be overturned by the one who raised Lazarus. Their Jewish worldview will be radically altered.

But there is another response to the raising of Lazarus. Some of those who witnessed the miracle return to Jerusalem to report the public spectacle of the miracle performed by Jesus. The chief priests and the Pharisees call for an emergency meeting. They decide, there and then, to put into motion what they have been contemplating for some time: to have Jesus arrested and executed. Do they do this because they do not believe Jesus could, in fact, work miracles? No! They decide to kill Jesus, not because they do not think the miraculous claims but because they are perfectly well aware of his unprecedented ability to work the supernatural. Based on their eyewitness experience, at least in a sense, they "believe" in Jesus as a worker of miracles. This belief in Jesus' miracles leads them to want to kill him.

Here is the point: We have two groups who are witnesses to the same event with an identical set of information about the event, yet we have wholly opposed responses. How can the same information produce diametrically opposite responses? The answer is that it depends on the lens through which one views the information. It depends on our information-interpretation filter. It depends on one's worldview. All of those present at the raising of Lazarus were Jews. Therefore, in principle, we might expect that all of them would have the same worldview, shaped by Judaism.

However, as we have already seen, there are two kinds of Jews here. First, there are those whose worldview has been shaken to the core by the life and ministry of Jesus of Nazareth. Everything they think they know about the relationship between Israel and Yahweh has been turned upside down. The Jewish presuppositions they grew up with are no longer in effect. If Jesus tells them that he is the resurrection and the life, it is true. It is true if he tells them he is the way, the truth, and the life. Their entire world, including their Jewish world, is interpreted through the life of the one who raised Lazarus. And in just a few short days, it will be interpreted through the life and the teachings of the one who was raised from the dead and ascended into heaven.

But what about the other group? What about the teachers of the Law, the Pharisees, and, presumably, others of the Jews who were at Bethany that day? How can they possibly have seen what Jesus did and not have "believed in him?" The answer is quite simple. They have a worldview shaped by Jewish presuppositions about the Jewish Messiah and the relationship between Yahweh and Israel. This produces an opposite response to Jesus' raising of Lazarus. From their worldview, the logical thing to do is to eliminate Jesus. To them, Jesus is a deceiver, a liar, a blasphemer, and a dangerous person. The fact that he raised Lazarus from the dead did not dispel them from this view. Not at all. It made him even more dangerous and sealed their decision to take action against him (John 11:47-53).

Let us remind ourselves how most Jews thought about their relationship as a people with their God and, more specifically, about the LORD's Messiah. The majority view of the Jews in the first century was that they were God's chosen people and would remain in this chosen-people status until the end of time. The idea that salvation is for the Gentiles too, which is foreshadowed in the Book of Jonah and prophesied in dozens of Old Testament passages, was not part of their view of God or of the world. This upstart from Galilee, with his message of love for our enemies and his description of a kingdom that is not of this world, which would include the Gentiles as equals with the Jews, could not have been true. No way!

Whatever Jesus' miracles do portend, it is not that he is the Messiah, that is for sure. We need an alternative explanation. Perhaps he is working through the power of Satan (Luke 11:15).

They have the same information but a radically different conclusion, and why? Because of a different view of the world. One group has had their eyes opened to be able to see a worldwide kingdom ruled by a spiritual king of both Jew and Gentile. The other sees through a Jews-only lens and reaches a radically opposed interpretation. This example proves that our worldview profoundly impacts how we interpret what we see and experience. It is worth bearing in mind that the worldview of the Jew and the

Christian are similar. They are nearly identical in many aspects, as both see the world through an assumption of non-deterministic monotheism. Yet, observe the radically different interpretations of the seemingly simple and obvious fact of the resurrection of Lazarus. It would be a great exercise to imagine a Hindu, an atheist, or a dualist being at Bethany that day, interpreting what they have seen and heard. What spin would they put on the raising of Lazarus by this Jesus from Nazareth? As an exercise, I suggest you do exactly that right now. Think about it and perhaps even write your answers down. We will be doing this exercise in chapter twelve of this book, but only after some of the other significant worldviews have been described.

The goal of this book is to help the reader to gain a solid understanding of the Christian and other worldviews and to understand why the Christian view of the world is, by far, with no close second, the superior view of reality. All other worldviews deceive us, send us in unhelpful directions, and do not make us the kind of people we want to be. To do this, I will first establish what a worldview is, and how our view of the world has such a controlling influence on our lives. Then I will do my best to define what a "good" worldview should look like. From there, I will analyze the principal worldviews we find among humanity today from the perspective of this idea of a "good" worldview.

ONE

What is a Worldview?

Our first step is to establish what a worldview is. I have already used a couple of metaphors to get us started. A worldview is like a pair of colored glasses. It is a lens through which information passes into our rational minds for us to interpret that data. Our worldview determines the meaning we derive from this information. Our worldview is composed of a set of presuppositions about the world. We think we are logical, intelligent, open-minded, and rational beings. Given the same array of information, we assume that any reasonable human being would arrive at the same or at least a similar conclusion from that information, something like the evidence in a court of law producing a finding beyond a reasonable doubt.

However, this assumption needs to be corrected. If we think that we view the world from an objective perspective, then we are deceiving ourselves. Even if our worldview is a correct one, it certainly is not an objective one. Responses to the raising of Lazarus are good evidence of this—the same information but radically different interpretations. Think for a moment about how most ancient people viewed the world. Anthropologists tell us that most were animists. They saw the world as a magical place, with spirits inhabiting the animals, the plants, the mountains, and the heavenly objects. Did they see lightning as we see lightning? No! They would have seen lightning as a manifestation of the wrath of a god or as the result of having failed to observe a taboo. Well, who was right about the cause of lightning, our aboriginal ancestor somewhere in the Australian outback or our rational, scientifically-informed modern mind? Who gets to decide which is the correct view? How do we know?

Of course, we tell ourselves that our view of lightning is correct, and in this case, it is demonstrably true. It is due to the buildup of static electricity as hot air rises and cold air sinks in clouds. But, whether we are determinists, Neoplatonists, dualists, pantheists, postmodernists, or deists, we naively and perhaps even pridefully assume that our view of questions about reality is correct. However, if we are humble and wise enough, we will realize that we need to be corrected about many things. What about the question of ultimate causes? What about more important questions than the cause of lightning, such as why we exist or what is the right thing to do? Can we assume, without investigating, that our view of such things is as reliable as our view of the cause of lightning? These are the fundamental human questions—value, purpose, meaning, right and wrong. It will be well worth delving deeply into an understanding of our worldview, analyzing our way of seeing reality, and learning how to base the way we live and think on a careful analysis of this question.

Still, we need a more formal definition of worldview. To establish this, let us step back just a bit. The fundamental question we are addressing is this: How do we know anything? There is a technical word that philosophers use to define the study of how we know what we know. It is the word *epistemology*. Here is one definition of epistemology from the authoritative source of all definitions, Wikipedia! Epistemology is "The theory of knowledge, especially about its methods, validity, and scope. Epistemology is the investigation of what distinguishes justified belief from opinion." How do we know what we know? For example, Christians believe that Jesus is the promised Messiah. How can we know if this is, in fact, true? Hopefully, you think that your mother loves you. How do you know, absolutely for sure, that she does love you? How do we know whether the world began in what we call the "big bang?" For that matter, how do we know that the earth is spinning?

Before the twentieth century, at least in the Western world, our modernist philosophers such as Francis Bacon, Renee Descartes, Isaac

Newton, and John Locke told us that we acquired objective, reliable knowledge about the nature of reality through an inductive and deductive approach to observation and reasoning. Induction involves viewing the world through direct observation and discovering patterns that define how things work. What are the patterns in the world? Those with helpful knowledge of such patterns we describe as wise. Deduction

Issac Newton (1643-1727)

involves starting with particular theories, beliefs, and assumptions and using those to predict the result of any specific set of events. We can then compare the prediction to actual data to decide if the theory is consistent. Observe a pattern, discover a law, create an approach to explain that law, and test the theory. If it works, then we are gaining fundamental knowledge of the world. To the enlightened modern, it was that simple.

More recently, our postmodern friends have rightly shown us that this simple rational approach to the world is fundamentally flawed. For example, Thomas Kuhn (1922-1996), a historian of science, shocked the world of rationalistic scientists by establishing that even scientists do not view the world nearly as rationally as we think. Our interpretation of even the most basic facts, such as scientific measurements, is absolutely and most fundamentally

Thomas Kuhn (1922-1996)

determined by our scientific paradigms, not by an open-minded rational analysis of indisputable facts. In his famous work, *The Structure of Scientific Revolutions* (1962), Kuhn demonstrated that our assumptions, even about how nature works, control how we interpret the most fundamental scientific observations about the world. Before the discovery of germ theory, scientists were utterly incapable of solving the most basic medical problems. Before the advent of the scientific paradigms known as quantum mechanics and relativity, scientists regularly and predictably completely misinterpreted almost every piece of information about how atoms, molecules, and stars work. Quantum Mechanics is a vastly superior scientific paradigm to Classical Mechanics (but to explain why that is true will require that I go into too many details, so please trust me on that).

I want to keep this analysis of epistemology—of how we know—simple for us. I will define three different levels of knowledge; three descriptions of how we acquire and interpret relatively reliable knowledge about how reality works. The three levels are theory, paradigm, and worldview. Of course, the critical term is a worldview, but let us build from theory to paradigm to worldview.

We will start with the idea of a theory. To quote from my textbook,

Introduction to Scientific Thought[1] "A theory is a cause and effect statement about the relationship between two variables." A theory is an explanation of a particular set of related data. The key word here is an explanation. Observation/induction tells us what happens, and theory tells us why it happens. Generally, a theory is a relatively narrow statement that predicts the outcome of a set of events in a narrowly defined situation. A "correct" theory is not necessarily "true," but one consistent with all or nearly all known examples. We can have a historical theory, a sociological theory, a business theory, or a theory about relationships. For instance, I notice that, generally, with birds, the males are more attractive than the females (unlike with humans). I theorize that this is because the females amongst birds choose their sexual partners. Or I might theorize that a particular set of psychological symptoms result from previous trauma. A theory attempts to explain why specific causes seem attached to certain effects. It helps us to organize our information about and understanding of the world. To live in the world, we have to theorize.

Karl Popper (1902-1994)

But, as Thomas Kuhn so wisely reminded us, and as the earlier philosopher of science, Karl Popper (1902-1994), told us, "knowledge is theory-laden." In other words, we think our theories are created from observation. We believe that our theories about the world are determined in some objective way by our unadulterated observation of the world. Philosophers such as Popper tell us we are wrong, and in this, they are right. This happens in science and any other area of human inquiry in which we develop explanatory theories. In other words, our approaches determine what we observe at least as much as our observations tell us what we theorize to explain those observations. If I theorize that taking a particular drug will resolve a specific symptom, then I observe that taking that drug fixes the predicted symptom. This is known as the placebo effect.

My favorite example of the placebo effect comes from an experiment

---

1   John M. Oakes, *Introduction to Scientific Thought*, (San Diego; cognella Press, 2015).

done in the 1990s on the food additive known as olestra.[2] Olestra was a fat substitute that tasted like fat. Still, because it was indigestible, it had virtually zero calories. It was the first commercially available low-calorie fat substitute—the fat-equivalent of sugar-substitutes such as aspartame (NutraSweet, Equal) or sucralose (Splenda). What a great idea—fat-calorie-free French fries, potato chips, and cookies that taste like the real thing. An experiment was done in which movie-goers were given snacks, some of which used vegetable oil, and others of which used olestra.

In this double-blind experiment, the intent was to see if olestra caused negative symptoms, especially diarrhea. Subjects were told that they might experience diarrhea because of eating the products, but they were not told whether they were in the test or the control group. Movie-goers who ingested olestra, not surprisingly, experienced a significant rise in symptoms of diarrhea. But here is the interesting result: Participants who had the vegetable oil products had a significant increase in symptoms of diarrhea as well. In other words, they got placebo effect/psychosomatic diarrhea simply because they believed they might! This fun story, though not so fun for the participants, illustrates an important point about theory, paradigm, and worldview. Our assumptions about how things work to a great measure determines how we interpret information. They also determine how we see ourselves.

Suppose our theories determine how we interpret the world. In that case, our paradigms do so much more significantly, as Thomas Kuhn told us and as many studies in a wide variety of human endeavors have proven. What is a paradigm? It is like a theory, but it covers a much wider field of knowledge. I will quote again from my *Introduction to Scientific Thought*:

> A paradigm is an underlying model or assumption which determines how discoveries are interpreted and what kind of questions are asked within a particular discipline.

A paradigm is more fundamental and broader in scope than a theory (and, as we will see, a worldview is still more foundational). A theory attempts to explain a relatively narrow set of observations, such as why we have an economic recession or why frog populations are dropping

---

2 https://pubmed.ncbi.nlm.nih.gov/9356283/

dramatically. A paradigm is a basic explanatory model for an entire discipline of study. One's paradigm determines what theories are put forth. Our economic paradigm determines our economic theories as much as or more than the evidence.

The history of science gives us good examples that both help us understand what a paradigm is and demonstrate how it influences our interpretation of data. Let us consider the field of geology. Before the late eighteenth century, geology was an immature science with no fundamental working paradigm. If there was a paradigm, it was the flood/cataclysm/ young earth model. However, this was never really a scientific paradigm, and it never was able to explain geological observations. Along came James Hutton

Charles Lyell (1797-1875)

(1726-1797), who, in his *Theory of Earth,* proposed that the earth was ancient. About its age, he boldly said, "No vestige of a beginning." He was followed up by Charles Lyell (1797-1875), who invented the uniformitarian model. He said, "The present is the key to the past." According to the uniformitarian geological model, gradual forces which are observable today, working over vast periods, determine the present state of the earth. Geology is not determined by cataclysms or by a recent creation.

Try to imagine how humans, especially in Europe, where this model was developed, viewed observables such as fossils, canyons, coal seams, mountains, and the like before the uniformitarian paradigm. The truth is that before this paradigm was developed, geologists had a very poor track record of explaining the available data. After the model was developed, all, or at least nearly all, data fit the model, allowing the modern science of geology to develop.

The first successful paradigm of physics was the classical model, mainly developed by Isaac Newton. It explained most of the available experimental evidence for about two hundred years. But, near the end of the nineteenth century, this paradigm collapsed as an ever-greater amount of data accumulated which the accepted model could not explain. Along came Albert Einstein, Max Plank, and others, who created the quantum model. It is hard to exaggerate how different the paradigm of quantum mechanics is from the classical model. Before this, chemistry had yet to successfully explain any of the fundamental properties of atoms and molecules. The currently-held theories to explain the properties of molecules using things such as quantum numbers would have been utter nonsense under the classical mechanics' paradigm.

No matter the paradigm regardless of whether it is a historical, sociological, economic, or psychological paradigm, the point is that the accepted model or paradigm determines the range of possible explanations of what we observe. Our paradigm tells us what we see, at least as much, if not more, than our eyes inform us. It tells us what kind of psychologist, educator, economist, lawyer, or farmer we will be. Data does not have unfettered access to an open mind. Our paradigms have a controlling effect on what we believe, whether we know this is true or not, and most of us are unaware of this controlling effect.

This brings us to our third "level" of knowledge: interpretation, our worldview. As our paradigm in a particular field determines our theories about that field of study, our worldview largely determines our paradigms. So, what is a worldview? As James W. Sire put it,[3] "A worldview is a set of presuppositions (i.e., assumptions) which we hold about the basic makeup of our world." As James Olthuis explains, "A worldview is a framework of a set of fundamental beliefs through which we view the world and our calling and future in it."[4] Or, even more simply, a worldview is the perspective one uses to process and interpret information received about the world. The point about a worldview is that it is a view of the whole world. In other words, our worldview does what a theory does with a narrow question and what a paradigm does for an entire field of study, but it does this to all of reality! It tells us how we should understand all information in all areas of inquiry. A worldview has a broad perspective. It determines the questions we ask about the universe and the answers we give to those questions.

To give a simple illustration, let us consider a possible personal theory, paradigm, and worldview. Let us think about how we view our mother. We might have a theory about her, a paradigm about her, and a worldview

---

3 James W. Sire, *The Universe Next Door* (Downer's Grove, IL: Intervarsity, 2009).

4 James H. Olthuis, "On Worldviews" from *Stained Glass: Worldviews and Social Science* (Lanham, MD: University Press of America, 1989)

under which we view her. You could use a new cell phone. You glimpse her search engine history and notice that your mother is looking into cell phones. You heard she was talking to a friend, asking about prices and models of cell phones. You decide on a theory. Your theory is that your mother is giving you a cell phone for Christmas. This is a reasonable explanation of the observations. Now we can do the experiment to test the theory. However, we will have to wait for Christmas.

But this theory is formed under an assumed paradigm about your mother. It is a paradigm that determines how you feel about your relationships. The paradigm is this: Your mother loves you. This is much bigger than a theory because whether your mother loves you or not has a fundamental impact on how you view yourself and relate to others. It also tells you to expect a thoughtful gift from your mother. Suppose you are deceived, and your mother is a manipulative, selfish person who only interacts with you for what she can gain. In that case, that will change the entire scope of how you view relationships generally and your self-worth, will it not? This paradigm also influences your theorizing. How you view the information about her use of social media and your mother's conversations with others is strongly influenced by your basic, unquestioned assumption that your mother truly loves you. If it turns out that she is a selfish, self-concerned narcissist, that changes how you interpret the information. Maybe she is just setting you up about the cell phone to let you down again. Perhaps she is jerking you around to get you to do something for her later. Or maybe she is just trying to get a cell phone for herself.

But this paradigm that your mother loves you is based on a worldview. As a Christian, I believe that love is more than just neurons firing and neurotransmitters being released at nerve synapses. Love, though not simply physical, is real. When love is experienced, it may result in the release of neurotransmitters, but it is a far more fundamentally real thing than a conditioned Pavlovian response. In fact, in my worldview, God is love. Love is real. Love is not a mere epiphenomenon. When I tell myself that my mother loves me, I mean that she loves me—that even if I cannot quantify that love, it is real. It is as real as her hair, her hands, and her eyes. In this simple example, we see that our view of the world has effects, even at the most granular level, on how we understand and live our lives daily. Because I believe that love is a real, actual thing, I am made able to use this understanding to predict that my mother will be buying me a cell phone for Christmas.

All of us have a worldview, even if we cannot delineate our view of the world. And all of us interpret the information we receive from the world through the lens of our worldview. This is how humans operate, and there is no escaping it. We can try to achieve intellectual ob-

Robert Kurka (1953-2018)

jectivity, which can work up to a point, but in the end, our worldview nearly always wins. As James Anderson put it, "A worldview is as indispensable for thinking as an atmosphere is for breathing." He also said about a worldview, "normally, you look through it rather than directly at it. It is essential, but it usually sits in the background of your thought."[5] As my good friend and mentor Robert Kurka (Long-term Professor at Lincoln Christian Univeristy) put it, "Worldviews provide their adherents with an **integrative story** that makes sense of their past, present, and future."[6]

What are these "presuppositions" that are a part of our worldview? They include the most basic ideas about how reality works. For example, we either assume that there is an ultimate moral authority or we do not. We either believe that the physical world is real or an ephemeral illusion (as some pantheists do). We either assume that the universe is eternal or that it is created. We either believe that our existence has meaning or that it is meaningless. We either think that humans have free will or that we live in a deterministic world. We either assume that there is a supernatural reality that overrides the natural, or we do not. It is not at all hard to see that our fundamental assumptions in these areas significantly impact what we do, what we believe, and how we behave. It determines almost everything that matters.

This raises a couple of essential questions. First, is it better to be aware of our worldview than to have only a vague, undefined idea of how we view the world? The answer is clearly yes. It is better to have a clearly understood view of how we see the world and how that affects every

5   James N. Anderson, *What's Your Worldview* (Wheaton, IL; Crossway, 2014), p. 13.
6   Robert Kurka, personal communication.

aspect of our values and what we do with the limited time and energy we have in this life. Many people, perhaps including ourselves, do not even have a name for our worldview. Having a name for our understanding of the world gives us clarity and helps us to find meaning in life. Of even more significant concern, we need a clear understanding of our worldview to articulate in simple propositions why we believe it is true. Some of us are walking through life in a fog—not knowing where we are going and why we are going there. No one wants to work at a job where the measures for success are not clearly defined. No one wants to participate in a game in which other players know the object of the game, but we do not. One primary goal of this book, then, is to help us to understand in clear terms what our worldview is.

A second question: Would it not be far better for us to understand why we believe what we believe—and the presuppositions underlying what we believe? Should we not find some basis for evaluating whether our worldview is a "good" one? Would it not be a good idea for each of us to examine our worldview to decide if it is really the view of the world that we want to hold on to? Maybe you grew up atheist or Hindu or part of a native religion, or, for that matter, a Christian theist. Is that where you want to land? Why? What is the criterion for each of us to know how we can best view the world? Even if you already feel good about your worldview, would you not want to understand it more deeply so that you can live more purposefully and explain it to others? And would you not want to have a solid grasp of other worldviews and why you choose to stick with the one you have chosen, even if you reject different worldviews? A second goal of this book is to help you to do this. What makes a worldview a "good" one? This is the subject of our next chapter.

TWO

True, Right, Better:
What is a Good Worldview?

Most of us think of ourselves as good people. We want to be good. We want to do what is right. Whether we succeed in being good people and doing what is right is another question, but I have yet to meet a person who sees themselves as bad. We have good intentions and want to live up to our fundamental understanding of what it means to be a good person.

This brings us to our next question. Our worldview, in considerable measure, defines who we are and what it means for us to be good. This begs the question: Is the worldview I hold to what I genuinely want to have as my entire set of assumptions of the world? Do I have a "good" worldview? Do I hold to the best possible view of the world?

Some might object that the best worldview is a matter of opinion or a highly subjective question. Perhaps they are right. How can we know which is the best worldview? And who has the right to say whose is the correct or the better set of assumptions about this world? "It's all relative," some might say, or "It's true for you but not for me." In this chapter, I want to propose a set of three qualities that I believe most anyone could accept as defining what would be a superior view of the world. This list of three measures of the goodness of a worldview is the source of the title of this book. In this chapter, I will define these three means of evaluating the integrity of a worldview and explain how they will be applied to the various worldviews that humans have devised. They are:

1. Is it true?
2. Is it right?
3. Is it better?

Is it true?

The first question is one that anyone could agree would help determine if a worldview is a good one. The question is this: Is this worldview true?

We can all agree that it is always better to be correct than to be in error. It is better to hold to a genuine belief than one that is false. We might debate whether any proposition is true or false, but all of us will agree that, generally speaking, being wrong on a question about the nature of reality is not good. In any human endeavor, there is no moral or practical advantage to being off the mark. Holding to the truth has few drawbacks, especially if it involves a philosophy about life.

One might object that being right about one's view of the world is subjective and a matter of opinion. What would it even mean for something so broad as a set of assumptions about reality to be "true?" Certainly, postmodernists will have a big problem with this kind of analysis, given that they view truth as relative or as being defined by those who hold to it. They do not accept the correspondence theory of truth (described below).

What, then, is a true worldview? I will be using the following definition: A "true" worldview is one which is consistent with everything we know about the reality of our universe. We may not be able to decisively "prove" that any one presupposition about the facts is true in a mathematical way similar to how we prove that an equilateral triangle has equal angles. However, we can ask whether a presupposition is consistent with what we know to be true from empirical observation of the universe. A "true" worldview is consistent with reality. No consistent observation of the universe disproves it. If a worldview includes a presupposition contradicted by well-known facts about the universe, then that presupposition, and presumably, that worldview is not valid.

For example, a worldview that could be used to predict that smoking cigarettes is good for your health would not be good because the evidence clearly shows that smoking is bad for one's health. A worldview from which one could interpolate that being selfish and self-centered is a good thing is not good because human experience tells us that selfishness is correlated with all kinds of mayhem, even with poor health and early death. An assumption about the universe that would lead us to predict that the laws of the universe are ever-changing would not be a correct view of the world. Why? Because all of our observations of the universe prove the opposite to be true. Empirical data confirms that the laws of the universe do not change over time. A worldview that predicts differently is not a true one. A worldview that can be used to "prove" that humans cannot travel to the planets is a false worldview because humans have visited the moon and will probably visit Mars in the next decade or so.

No matter your view of the world, even if you are not sure what that worldview is, surely you will agree that it is better to hold to a truth about the universe than a falsehood. Even if we occasionally prefer to believe a lie for personal reasons (something quite common in my experience), all will agree, at least in principle, that it is better for one's belief to be true than for it to be false.

Augustine of Hippo (354-430 AD)

An example of an untrue worldview comes to mind. It is from the life of the Christian bishop and theologian Augustine of Hippo (354-430 AD). Augustine was raised in a Christian home. His mother, Monica, was a devoted believer with great expectations for her precocious son. Despite her efforts, Augustine went off the rails as a youth, descending into wild living in Carthage. When he came to his senses, he began a spiritual journey that brought him not directly to Christianity but to Manicheism. This dualist religion began in Persia, with solid ascetic tendencies. Manicheism was founded by its supposedly inspired teacher Mani. Necessary for our discussion, the Manichees had a particular cosmology. According to Mani, the waxing and waning of the moon was not merely the reflection of light from a distant celestial object. The waxing of the moon was caused by the influx of released fragments of "light" flowing upward from the earth. Augustine was a student of natural philosophy. He found the Manichean cosmology to conflict with astronomical observations. Expressing his skepticism about Manicheism's cosmology to his peers, he was told that the great teacher of their religion, Faustus, would be able to answer his questions.

Faustus of Milevis came to Carthage in 383 AD, eight years after Augustine's conversion. The young convert eagerly expected the wise teacher of the Manichee religion to be able to clear up the apparent cosmological inconsistency involving the moon. He eventually won an audience with a great teacher. Unfortunately, when Augustine asked Faustus to explain how their belief about the waxing and waning of the moon could be explained, he was instead rebuked for his lack of faith. Augustine's comment: "I found in him [Mani] no reason given for the solstices and the equinoxes or the eclipses of the sun and the moon or anything else of this kind which I had learned in the books of secular [natural] philosophy. I was told to believe in these views of Mani, but they did not correspond with what had been established by mathematics and my eyesight. They were widely divergent."[7] Augustine reasoned that if Mani claimed to be an inspired teacher, yet made testable "false statements" about the heavens, then his claims to be "a divine person" were untrue. Notice, Augustine's test of the Manichee worldview was whether its claims were consistent. Did they "correspond" with known facts about the physical universe? If not, then the teachings and the worldview of Mani were false. Within a year, he rejected the Manichee worldview and left the religion. His conclusion: A religion that makes demonstrably false statements about reality is a false religion. The same can be said for a worldview. Concerning his former faith, Augustine said, "Food in dreams is exactly like real food, yet it does not sustain us, for we are only dreaming."[8]

Is It Right?

Our second measure of the "goodness" of a worldview is whether it is correct. What I mean is this. Does this worldview give good, reasonable, "right" answers to the most basic questions humans care about? If a worldview does not provide satisfactory answers to life's most basic questions, then it is not a good one. Of course, this begs the question: What are these so-called vital questions that a religion or a worldview must answer rightly? What questions must any good worldview successfully address?

To answer this question, I will turn to a class I have taught many times as a science professor. The version I taught at Grossmont College in San Diego is titled "Intro to Scientific Thought." One of the subjects addressed in this class is the relationship between science and religion. I talk about what science is and what it does and propose what religious beliefs in their most general sense are and what faith does. In the discussion, I propose to the students that science is, by far, the most successful means ever devised by human beings to answer a particular set of questions. The questions science answers with great success are as follows:

---

7 Augustine, Confessions, V.3.
8 Augustine, Confessions, III.6.

How big is that thing?
What is its mass?
How long does a particular process take?
What is the cause of a particular effect?
When? Where? How Many? By what means?

Religion is not very good at answering these questions. Neither is philosophy. How old is the earth? How do stars work? How do living things reproduce? Science is good at answering these questions. I tell my students that science answers questions about why (small w) but does not answer questions about Why (capital W). Why does the rock fall to the earth? Because of gravity. Why does gravity exist? Because of gravitons, or perhaps it has to do with the Higgs boson. Why are there Higgs bosons? We can keep going backward, asking why (little w) questions, but eventually, we come to Why? Why are there gravitons? Why do they exist at all, as opposed to them not existing? This is the existential, the essential question of why, not a question about the cause of a thing, but the reason for the item itself. Here science is useless.

Here is the point. Does anyone care all that much about questions such as where, when, how many, and by what means? Do we get up in the morning to answer when, where, or how many? The answer is no. These are not the essential questions of life. A good worldview does not need to answer these questions. What, then, are the questions that a successful worldview must provide good, sound, reasonable, and satisfactory answers to? Let me propose a list:

Why am I here?
What is my purpose?
How did I get here?
What is my value?
What is a human being?
What is the right thing to do?
Is or will there be ultimate justice?
What is the nature of ultimate reality?
What happens to me when I die?

The question "What is a human being?" deserves an explanation. Is a human merely a container composed of cells, neurons, and neurotransmitters, or am I more than mere chemicals? Is there any real meaning to ideas such as self-awareness and free will? Do "I" exist? Other important questions include the following: Does human history have any purpose or ultimate direction, or is history merely a record of random, human-caused events? If there is a supernatural reality, does the supernatural interact in the physical world or in human affairs? Why is there suffering in the world? Why is there evil in the world?

These are the questions that all human beings, be they atheists, dualists, animists, theists, pantheists, or any other "ists," want to be answered. Some worldviews may appear to diminish the importance of one or more of these questions. As we will see, Buddhism, or at least Buddha himself, downplayed the significance of the question of ultimate reality. Atheists try to reduce or even eliminate questions about morality. However, it is my personal experience that actual Buddhists care about ultimate truth and flesh and blood atheists and agnostics, at their core, care deeply about right and wrong, even if they formally disagree with what their hearts tell them.

Here is the point: A "good" worldview will provide reasonable, satisfactory, believable answers to questions about the value of human beings, their purpose (if any), what is the right thing for them to do in any particular situation, and so forth. These answers will be consistent with other things we know about reality. For example, if the purpose for humans that a particular worldview proposes is impossible for humans to actually achieve, then that would not be a "good" answer to the question of purpose. If a worldview tells us that a particular behavior is immoral, when everything humans know from their hearts to be true tells them that it is moral, we may need to question that worldview. We will see that the different worldviews vary widely in their success at answering these questions.

Of the three questions we will apply to the different worldviews, this second question is the most difficult to evaluate. One can argue that of the three questions—true, right, and better—whether a worldview is right is the most subjective to apply. On the other hand, I would argue that it may also be the most important of the three for us to answer because, as already stated, these are the most fundamental questions that all human beings, no matter their worldview, really want to find answers to. This is what we care about. It is what makes us tick and keep on ticking. It is why we get up in the morning and stay up late at night.

Is It Better?

The third question we will be using to evaluate the goodness of the various worldviews is this: Is this worldview better than others? What I mean is this. Given what we know about the basic precepts of any given worldview, can we reasonably predict that a person holding consistently to this worldview will therefore be a better person for living in a way consistent with that worldview than he or she might otherwise have been? In asking this question, we assume that a person holds firmly to the assumptions of their worldview and lives a life consistent with the beliefs about reality associated with that view of the world. This is a big assumption, but it is only fair to evaluate a worldview as "better" on the presumption that a believer in that worldview lives consistently with their beliefs. Does postmodernism, lived consistently, produce better people than pantheism? Does deism produce better people than atheism or theism?

The skeptics among us (hopefully, all of us) are screaming out now. What do you mean by better? Would this not be circular reasoning? Doesn't the worldview itself define what a better person is? Who gets to decide what makes for a "better" person?

My response to this is that the question of what worldview is better is more straightforward to ask and answer than you might think. I would argue that this is a relatively straightforward question and that consensus on what is a "better" person could be achieved quite easily. I propose that if we put a Muslim, a Hindu, a Buddhist, an animist, an atheist, a dualist, and a person who has no idea what her worldview is into a room and task this group to come up with a consensus description of what makes for a "good" person, they would find that task relatively easy.

Let me propose that you do this activity right now. Imagine the list of qualities that make for a good person for yourself. Propose a list of qualities of a good person which you believe are not necessarily produced by your personal assumptions about the world but one which you and your neighbors could agree on. Try to do this without letting your religious perspective come into play. Imagine you are in the room I just described and are asked to come up with your first draft of the qualities of a good person. You will probably come up with a list something like this:

humble
generous
courageous
diligent
self-controlled
honest
self-sacrificing
compassionate
peace-loving

The classic Greek culture produced a set of seven virtues. They were humility, charity, chastity, gratitude, temperance, patience, and diligence. If we look at Buddha's eightfold path, the list is quite similar. The eight paths of Buddhism are right understanding, right thought, right speech, right action, right livelihood, right effort, right mindfulness, and right concentration. And, yes, our atheist friends will also have a similar list. I conclude that of the three questions we will apply to the various worldviews in play amongst humans, the third question—whether a particular worldview, if followed consistently, will produce a better person—will be the easiest to evaluate.

We will ask this kind of question: Can we reasonably predict that a pantheist will be more generous, a theist will be more honest, or an atheist will be more self-controlled than one who holds to an alternative worldview? As with the previous two questions, we will find that different worldviews will fare far differently from others in this regard. In fact, let me give away the answer before we start. Christianity will outshine all opposing worldviews in this: If a human consistently lives out the implications of the Christian worldview, they will be the best person they can possibly be, with the other worldviews rather far in the rearview mirror. But I get well ahead of myself here.

THREE

What is the Christian Worldview?

In this chapter, I will attempt to describe and explain the Christian view of the world. I will delay the application of our three evaluative questions to the Christian worldview until chapter eleven. In this chapter, I will describe but not evaluate the Christian worldview. In the succeeding chapters, I will describe and explain the various other worldviews and, at the same time, apply our three questions to them: Are they true, right, and better? Only after evaluating the different worldviews, will we return to assess the Christian understanding of reality according to our three criteria. Is the Christian worldview true, right, and better?

Let us ask ourselves this: What is the Christian worldview? We are not asking about Christian doctrine or Christian practice. We are asking more fundamental questions than this. We are asking the following: What does Christianity have to say about the nature of reality? What is the universe, and what is true in and about the universe if Christianity is true?

Let me challenge the reader to do this exercise. You are being asked to do something that most Christians rarely, if ever, do. Or if they do it, they need to be made aware that they are doing it at the time. It is not the habit of most Christians (or most humans) to ask what is the nature of reality. And even if we ask ourselves questions about the nature of reality, as believers, we may not look at these most fundamental questions through the lens of the Bible.

Imagine, then, you are trying to describe the Christian idea of reality to a person who knows nothing about Christianity or the Christian Scriptures. In doing so, you will anticipate answering the essential human questions in section two above. But you will do this without direct reference to much of biblical history and Christian doctrine, because the person you are speaking to knows nothing of these things.

I have spent considerable time reflecting on this question. In doing so, I have found that I need only go as far as the first four chapters of

Genesis to answer the question: What is the Christian view of the world? If I am right, the Christian view of the world is virtually identical to the Jewish worldview. Almost every point I am about to make below about the Christian worldview can be extracted from Genesis chapter One.

What is the first chapter of Genesis about? It is, in essence, a description of the biblical worldview. In the opening chapter of the Christian and Jewish Scripture, God introduces himself to humanity. Here is who I am, and here is what I am about. Scholars tell us that Genesis chapter one is a polemic in which the Hebrew God explains who he is while, at the same time, arguing against the Babylonian worldview—the common worldview in Mesopotamia in roughly 2000 BC. More specifically, scholars have proposed that Genesis chapter one is a polemic against the Babylonian creation myth, the *Enumah Elish*.[9] In his commentary on Genesis, Gordon Wenham has described the prologue of Genesis as follows: "Genesis 1-11 is a commentary, often highly critical, on ideas current in the ancient world about the natural and supernatural world."[10] In the *Enumah Elish*, humanity is an afterthought of the gods. They play a relatively minor role in the grand scheme of things. In the Babylonian worldview, the purpose of humans is to serve the gods. Genesis one turns this view of the world on its head. In the Genesis story, human beings are not on the periphery but at the heart of the story. In Genesis, humans were created not to serve the gods' needs but so that the one true God could have a relationship with us. What a striking contrast!

I have taught the book of Genesis in several settings. In doing so, I have described the following summary of the entire biblical story:

Genesis 1	Who is God?
Genesis 2	Who are we?
Genesis 3-11	We have a big problem with God.
Genesis 12-Revelation 20	God is fixing the problem.
Revelation 21-22	God has solved the problem.

What, then, is the biblical view of the world, and how can we find this worldview in the first chapters of Genesis? The following is a basic

---

9   For example, Paul Copan and Douglas Jacoby, *Origins* (Spring, TX: Illumination Publishers, 2018)
10   Gordon J. Wenham, *Genesis 1-15*, World Bible Commentary, Vol. 1 (Waco, TX; Word Books, 1987), p. xlvii.

description that I have used of the Christian worldview:

1. The physical world is a) real, b) created out of nothing (*ex nihilo*), and c) essentially good.

2. There exists an unseen spiritual reality that is not limited to or defined by physical reality. Human beings have a spiritual and physical aspect to their nature.

3. The creator of the physical and spiritual realms is the God who reveals himself in the Bible.

4. Certain qualities characterize God. He is a person. He is love. He is good. He is just. He is holy, sovereign, omniscient, omnipotent, and omnipresent.

5. Although all of God's creation is good, evil exists. Evil is the result of a rebellion by persons with a free will against the will of their Creator.

6. Because of God's justice and holiness, those who rebel against him will ultimately be judged and separated from God for eternity.

7. God's love solves the solution to the problem of evil and eternal separation from God through the atoning sacrifice of Jesus Christ.

Let us look at the first chapters of Genesis and see this worldview revealed in an amazingly succinct story of creation. The Genesis story begins with these words: "In the beginning." Right away, we have an essential statement about reality. The physical universe had a beginning. Before the beginning, nothing was that is (John 1:1, Colossians 1:15-17, Hebrews 1:2). Does Genesis 1:1 imply creation *ex nihilo* (creation of everything, literally out of nothing at all)? We will let the scholars debate the fine points here, but let me give my opinion: Yes! And even if it is not unquestionably established in the Genesis creation account, it is made clear in the other passages referenced above. To the Christian, this first point about the Christian worldview may seem obvious, but we will see that other worldviews are not consistent with a universe created out of nothing by a personal God. In some worldviews, God coexists with the universe; therefore, God could not have created the universe out of nothing.

"In the beginning." Next, we have "In the beginning God...." Our first point from the Genesis story is that there was a beginning. Our second point is that God pre-existed the universe. God is an eternal and uncreated being. And in Genesis chapter one, God speaks ("And God said..."), meaning that God is a person, not an impersonal force. God is the pre-existent One. God is the personal, uncaused cause. The uncaused cause of what?

"In the beginning." "In the beginning, God." *"In the beginning, God created the heavens and the earth... and the Spirit of God was hovering over the waters."* God is the uncaused cause of the physical universe and of the unseen spiritual realm as well. Here we see revealed another layer of the biblical worldview. God is the pre-existent one, and the Creator of the physical reality (the heavens and the earth) and of spiritual reality as well. His Spirit hovers over the waters. He is a spiritual being. He is not a physical being. Given his power to create everything out of nothing, he is omnipotent, and given that he is hovering over the waters, he is omniscient and omnipresent. We will look at the different worldviews in the subsequent chapters, but suffice it to say that if Genesis 1:1 is true, then animism, polytheism, pantheism, dualism, atheism, and, indeed, nearly all the competing isms are already proven false.

Of course, one of our tasks in this book is to ask whether Genesis 1:1 is true. At this point, the only competing worldview left standing, other than theism, is deism, but even deism is holding on by its fingernails. It will be pushed off the ledge in Genesis 2. By the way, for the record, there is one worldview other than Judaism or Christianity which is still in play, which is the Muslim worldview. The Islamic view of the world will come up against Genesis chapter three shortly.

The first four points of the Christian worldview have nearly been established in Genesis 1:1-3. Still, two fundamental aspects of the biblical description of reality remain to be established by the first chapter of Genesis. *"Then God said, 'Let us make mankind in our image, in our likeness, so that they may rule over the fish in the sea and the birds in the sky'...."* Here we see the unique nature of God's crowning creation. Human beings are created in the image of God. There is a lot to be unpacked here, but we will limit ourselves to just a few implications for now. Humans, being made in God's image, have physical and spiritual aspects. We are not simply a bag of bones. Humans are the crown of God's creation and the purpose for which the universe was created. This is the biblical view of humanity.

Finally, there is Genesis 1:31. *"God saw all that he had made, and it was very good."* It is hard to overstate the significance of this simple statement in the biblical creation story and the chasm it leaves between the biblical worldview and that of its competitors. Creation is good. Full stop. Everything created by the God of Genesis 1 is good. In fact, it is very good. This will create problems for the defense of the Christian worldview as we proceed. Why? Because as we look around us, we can see that in our present reality, not all is good. Yet, the biblical view is that everything God created is very good. Part of our defense of the Christian worldview will be an explanation of this dichotomy.

Having established in Genesis chapter one the first four points of the Christian worldview as delineated above, the following three chapters of Genesis serve to bring out points five through seven. Adam and Eve are in a perfect, harmonious, intimate relationship with the God who created them. They are in a garden where all their needs are met. But God gives them a choice. Why? Because God is love, and love always gives a choice. Love cannot be forced. In fact, what would love even mean in a world without beings who have free will? And the choice had to be a real one. The alternative to living in harmonious submission to our Creator had to be a viable alternative. It could not be a choice between a million dollars and a punch in the nose. The alternative to complete submission to God's will for us was very attractive. If not, would it even have been a choice, and would free will even have had meaning?

The rest, as they say, is history. Or, to be more precise, it is biblical history. We used our freedom as an opportunity to rebel, and even if we did not fully understand it at the time, our rebellion produced terrible consequences. Why? Because God is love, but he is also holy and just. His holiness can have nothing to do with sin and doers of evil. The result was separation from God—metaphorically, we all lost our place in the garden. *"So, the Lord God banished him from the Garden of Eden"* (Genesis 3:23).

By the end of Genesis chapter three, we have established points five and six in the biblical worldview described above. But what about point number seven? What about redemption and the opportunity to return to the garden? What about those holy, righteous, and mighty cherubim who are now preventing our return to an intimate relationship with a holy God? (Genesis 3:24). What is to be done about that?

Chapters three and four of Genesis contain subtle hints of the biblical solution to the problem of evil. God said to the serpent in the garden, *"And I will put enmity between you and the woman, and between your offspring and hers; he will crush your head and you will strike his heel"* (Genesis 3:15). The enemy—the tempter and deceiver whose pernicious influence played so significant a role in our being ejected from the Garden—will eventually be crushed. Whether the "he" of this passage is a reference to the Christian messiah is debatable, but the result is not. Mankind will be presented with a way back into intimate fellowship with his/her Creator. Other hints are found in Genesis 4:15-16, in which God provides gracious protection to Cain from the consequences of his sin, and in Genesis 4:25-26, in which Adam and Eve are given a third son—one who begins the painfully long process of sinful humans calling on the name of the Lord.

There is so much of the biblical story left out of this picture, but the basic Christian view of the world is established in the first four chapters of Genesis. This is the view that we will be comparing other worldviews to, and it is the view of the world that we will be evaluated for whether it is true, right, and better in a future chapter. We will now turn to a discussion of the competing worldviews proposed and accepted by our fellow human beings.

FOUR

Other Worldviews

I am a relatively older person. To be specific, I am an older white male American. I began college fifty years ago. I may be overgeneralizing and sentimental here, but the way I remember it, things were simpler back then. What I mean is this: I grew up in an unabashedly Judeo-Christian world. I had a couple of Jewish friends growing up in suburbia, but until well into my 20s, I had zero interaction with Buddhists, Hindus, or Muslims. The people I knew were either nominally Christians or non-believers who had grown up around Christianity. I was not a committed Christian. In fact, for a time early in my university days, I claimed to be an atheist. In any case, from my youth, I had been immersed in a Christian worldview, and I was only vaguely aware of other lenses used for looking at the world.

Here we are fifty years later. In the United States, the experts tell us that we have entered the post-Christian age. Europe was ahead of us in this, but in America, we have reached the tipping point at which we can no longer assume the majority we meet on campus or at work accept the Christian viewpoint of the world. In my neighborhood, I run into Muslims, Sikhs, Buddhists, and even animists (we have a number of Hmong in the area). Yoga, a Hindu practice, is a favored form of exercise, and Vedic forms of meditation are popular. Recent studies show that the fastest growing group in America, especially among the young, are the nones. These people say they are spiritual yet do not associate with any particular spiritual tradition. To the extent that Hollywood presents a worldview, for example, in the *Star Wars* world or *Pandora,* it appears to be vaguely Buddhist or Hindu. The nones I interact with tend in this direction as well. Their worldview is somewhere between postmodernism and pantheism. Many have leanings that would have been described as New Age a generation ago. When I share my faith on campus (something I do a lot), the biggest group is still Christian believers or nominal believers, but this position is eroding fairly quickly. Unlike when I was a college student, I cannot assume that those I meet know who Moses and Abraham are. They are far more likely to know about Lebron James than Saint James.

The Christian worldview is no longer a shared viewpoint in the Western world, and for me to share the gospel with people, I cannot simply assume a basic background in Christianity. It has reached the point that to bring Christian belief to people, I need to begin by explaining some of the essential elements of the Christian worldview. For example, I often engage in conversations in which I explain that God is good and, despite any appearances to the contrary, his creation is also very good. The idea of ultimate authority for truth has eroded significantly, to the point that many do not agree that there is any ultimate authority at all. In the same conversation, I am compelled to explain why evil exists.

We can bemoan the demise of the Christian worldview, but I do not. I think about the tremendous growth of the early Christian church in a world that was about as far from accepting the Christian worldview as one can imagine, yet Christianity did very well in this setting. Historically, Christianity appears to do at least as well from a minority position as it does when favored by the majority. Part of me is sentimental about Christianity having lost its unquestioned favored position, but a greater part of myself is encouraged to keep up the good fight, despite the odds. However, in the present situation, a Christian believer had better be prepared to present, explain and defend the Christian worldview. I hope this book has a measurable impact in meeting this need.

Among those who do Christian apologetics, there are several views on the most effective approach. A helpful book on this topic is *Five Views on Apologetics*.[11] The classic view, which is that of Thomas Aquinas, is that the first step in convincing people of Christianity is to prove the reality of the existence of a personal God. The method of apologetics I was introduced to in the first three decades of my life as a believer is variously known as evidential apologetics or cumulative case apologetics. This is the approach I have used the most in my work as an apologist. I have authored a book that takes this approach. It is *Reasons for Belief*.[12] This approach involves presenting a case for the inspiration of the Bible through

11   Steven B. Cowan, Ed., *Five Views on Apologetics* (Grand Rapids, MI: Zondervan, 2000)

12   John M. Oakes, *Reasons for Belief: A Handbook of Christian Evidence* (Spring, TX: Illumination Publishers, 2005).

various sources of evidence such as messianic prophecy, evidence for the resurrection, arguments involving the claims of Jesus, archaeology, science, and more.

In the America of the 1970s or the Europe of 1940, this approach was relatively effective simply because those we were sharing with had a fundamental outlook favorable to the idea of a personal God who speaks with authority. Cumulative case apologetics can still be helpful, but we are fast approaching a time when, arguably, the most effective means to convince non-believers in many parts of the world will be what is sometimes called presuppositional apologetics or worldview apologetics. This book is, in essence, a worldview apologetic. A worldview apologetic involves presenting the most commonly accepted set of worldview presuppositions and arguing for the relative cogency, effectiveness, and consistency of the various worldviews in light of human reality.

In this chapter, I will briefly introduce the other worldviews we will interact with in the post-Christian age, as well as a couple of less common world-viewing lenses. There are about as many ways to organize a study of worldviews as there are authors on the subject. Below I will present three I have found helpful and introduce how our discussion of various worldviews will be organized.

The first division of worldviews is from the work of a good friend and mentor, Robert Kurka. Dr. Kurka groups all the various ways of viewing reality into three bundles.

1. **Theism:** The basic view of the world which believes in a personal Creator who is separate from the created order:
   a. Biblical Theism
   b. Deism
   c. Theistic Existentialism
   d. Islamic Theism

2. **Pantheism:** All reality is, ultimately, One.
   a. Eastern pantheistic monism (Hinduism, Buddhism, etc.)
   b. Animism/Occult
   c. New Age
   d. Polytheism

3. **Naturalism:** Only the natural is real. There is no supernatural realm.
   a. Secular Humanism
   b. Marxism
   c. Nihilism
   d. Atheistic existentialism
   e. Postmodernism (no worldview is the correct one)

A second organization of worldviews is that of James Sire, the author of what many consider to be the "Bible" of worldview texts for beginners, *The Universe Next Door*.

James Sire (1933-2018)

Christian Theism
Islamic Theism
Deism
Naturalism
Nihilism
Existentialism
Eastern Pantheistic Monism
Postmodernism

A third arrangement of worldviews is that of James N. Anderson. His book on the subject is *What's Your World View?* In this easy-to-read book, Anderson uses a series of basic questions which will allow anyone to decide for themselves what their or anyone else's worldview is. His list of worldviews is more complete than the others. It is not as systematically arranged, and it includes some rare worldviews.

Dualism
Idealism (the only things which are real are of the mind)
Christianity
Deism
Finite Godism (a personal God who is limited in power)
Islam
Judaism
Materialism
Monism (everything is ultimately One)
Mysticism (a personal God who only reveals himself personally)
Nihilism (everything is meaningless)

Panentheism (the universe is contained in an impersonal God)
Pantheism (the universe is God)
Platonism
Pluralism
Polytheism
Relativism (postmodernism)
Skepticism
Unitarianism

So, what will be our organizational approach for evaluating the various worldviews? I have been a college student, a college professor, and a campus minister for the last fifty years. Therefore, in this book, I will be evaluating worldviews more or less in descending order of those that I deal with in my outreach to college students. My approach is more of a practical one than a systematic one. In the appendix, I will handle minor worldviews such as nihilism, existentialism, and Marxism. Here is our approach:

Christian Theism (already described but evaluated later)
Naturalism/Atheism
Postmodernism
Animism/Polytheism/Dualism
Pantheism/Eastern Religion/New Age
Deism
Islamic Theism

Let us begin.

FIVE

Naturalism/Atheism

The first worldview we will evaluate has many labels. It has been called naturalism, scientific materialism (or simply the possibly confusing label materialism), determinism, scientism, and atheism. Worldview scholars do not like the label atheism because it is too narrow a word to describe an entire worldview. They argue that it is simply the rejection of a single notion and is not a belief system. This distinction is not our concern. For most people, this is the word they apply to those with a wholly naturalistic worldview. We will use the terms above interchangeably. Atheism has never been a majority view at any time in human history. Even in officially atheist states like the former Soviet Union or Red China, it is not likely that it was ever a majority view. We are covering this worldview first for a couple of reasons. First, as a professor of science, it is one that I am particularly likely to come across, and it is one I must frequently respond to. Second, it is a very simple worldview to define and evaluate, making it an excellent first candidate for our true, right, better analysis.

What, then, is naturalism or scientific materialism? It is the presupposition that the only things which are real are observable, measurable, natural things. It is the assumption that there is no supernatural reality. The materialist believes that only physical entities are real. Spiritual, moral, and metaphysical things are not real. At best, they are epiphenomena—the result of complex physical realities. They only appear to be real. For example, if determinists are correct, then human consciousness is only an epiphenomenon. Even our very selves—our identity as persons—are not real. We are purely physical beings, made up of atoms, molecules, cells, and tissues which respond to the information stored in neurons, mediated by neurotransmitters. If naturalism is an accurate description of reality, then what we are as human beings is merely the result of our physical bodies interacting with our environment. Free will is a meaningless term in this worldview. If naturalism is a correct view of the world, then we cease to exist when we die. If the only things which are real are natural, physical entities, then the idea of life after death is an illusion. Let us consider a few statements of determinism from people who hold to this view.

First, listen to Julian Huxley, evolutionary biologist and atheist: "We are as much the product of blind forces as is the falling of a stone to earth, or the ebb and flow of the tides. We have just happened, and man was made flesh by a long series of singularly beneficial accidents."[13] Note the ironic appropriation of John 1:14.

Or we can consider the statement of Francis Crick, the co-discoverer of the double-helical structure of DNA: "The Astonishing Hypothesis is that you—your joys and your sorrows, your memories and your ambitions, your sense of personal identity and free will, are no more than the behavior of a vast assembly of nerve cells and their associated molecules."[14]

A more up-to-date statement of scientific materialism is that of the famous evolutionist and atheist Richard Dawkins: "In the universe of blind physical forces and genetic replication, some people are going to get hurt, and other people are going to get lucky: and you won't find any rhyme or reason to it, nor any justice. The universe we observe has precisely the properties we should expect if there is at the bottom, no design, no purpose, no evil, and no good. Nothing but blind, pitiless indifference. DNA neither knows nor cares. DNA just is, and we dance to its music."[15] Or, as Carl

Richard Dawkins

Sagan said, "The Cosmos is all that is or ever was or ever will be."[16]

Most helpful for our purposes is a statement by Richard Lewontin: "We exist as material beings in a material world, all of whose phenomena are the consequences of material relations among material entities. In a word, the public needs to accept materialism, which means that they must put God in the trash can of history where such myths belong."[17]

13   Anthony Smith, *The Human Degree* (J. B. Lippincott Co, 1976)

14   Daniel Voll, "Soul Searching with Francis Crick, *Omni* (February 1994), 46.

15   Richard Dawkins, *River Out of Eden: A Darwinian View of Life* (Harper Collins, 1995).

16   James W. Sire, *The Universe Next Door* (Downer's Grove, IL: Intervarsity, 2009), p. 51.

17   Richard Lewontin, "Billions and Billons of Demons" *New York Review of Books,* January 9, 1997, 31.

Atheism is mostly a recent phenomenon in human history. Surely there were true atheists in the ancient world, but they made little impact on people's daily lives. Few, if any, writings of *bona fide* atheists have come down to us. Aristophanes (c. 448–380 BC) wrote in his play *The Knights:* "Shrines! Shrines! Surely you don't believe in the gods. What's your argument? Where's your proof?"[18] Plato was accused of being an atheist, but he vigorously denied the charge. Both he and his contemporary Aristophanes rejected Greek polytheism but not the idea of the supernatural. Platonism is akin to what we will describe as panentheism.

How did we get here? If pure naturalism is a recent phenomenon, what was its genesis? The answer is that, historically, atheism/naturalism is the result of the coming together of science and the Age of Reason in the seventeenth century in Europe. The following is a brief history of how skepticism and even atheism arose in Christian Europe.

In the late Roman and early Medieval period, due to the influence of Platonism and Neoplatonism on Christian thinkers such as Augustine, a kind of dualism entered into Christianity, especially in Western Europe. This is the idea that physical things are essentially evil. Only higher, non-physical things are good or even worthy of our attention. This partially explains effects such as the call for the celibacy of priests. Before about the twelfth century, for an educated person to study the physical world was to debase oneself. Theology reigned as the queen of the sciences. Natural philosophy—the systematic study of the physical world—was ignored in Christian Europe. But with theologians such as Albertus Magnus and Thomas Aquinas, Western theologians turned away from Plato and toward Aristotle. Common sense philosophers such as Aquinas began to notice that the Bible declares all of creation to be good—very good (Genesis 1:31).

By the thirteenth century, philosophers/theologians such as Roger Bacon (c. 1240-1292) began to propose the idea of general revelation—that God reveals himself in limited ways to human beings through his physical creation. Bacon said, "The result of all true philosophy is to arrive at a knowledge of the Creator through knowledge of the created world."[19]

---

18 *Classic Drama Plays by Greek, Spanish, French, German and English Dramatists ...* – Albert Ellery Bergh. August 2004. ISBN 9781417941865.

19 Roger Bacon, *Opus Majus*, 1267.

It is difficult for us in the modern world to understand how revolutionary a break with the Christian past this was. Bacon proposed that a single, unchanging God created a single set of common physical laws which govern the universe and that these laws should be mathematical in their beauty and understandable by humans made in God's image. This proposal has proved to be spectacularly successful in the succeeding eight centuries. Bacon said that these physical laws could be discovered through "external experience, aided by instruments, made precise by mathematics."[20] In other words, he proposed what we now call the scientific method as a means of discovering the underlying order in nature he predicted to exist from his theology.

In the fourteenth century, William of Ockham (c. 1285-1349) proposed an empirical approach to acquiring knowledge of the created world and understanding the implications of Christian theology. He suggested what is called Ockham's Razor, which is the idea that the simplest explanation—one that requires fewer assumptions—is the best explanation of any empirical observation. This "razor" became the means by which philosophers eventually excluded the supernatural from explaining how the natural world functions. No longer were angels invoked to explain the motion of planets. To Ockham, nature normally behaves naturally, not supernaturally.

By the fifteenth century, such inquiry began to bear fruit as the Polish natural philosopher Nikolai Copernicus (1473-1542) used his empirical observations of the planets to overturn the medieval cosmological model of geocentrism—which had put the earth at the center of the universe. With Copernicus, the earth, and therefore the humans on the earth, were no longer at the center of God's creation but on a relatively small planet, circling at a great

Nikolai Copernicus (1473-1542)

distance a much larger sun. Copernicus was succeeded by Galileo (1564-1642), who made science an activity performed in a laboratory using controlled experiments. Galileo wisely said, "The Bible was written to tell us how to go to heaven, not how the heavens go."[21] Concerning general

20 Ibid.
21 Galileo Galilei, "Letter to the Grand Duchess Christina of Tuscany," in John Oakes, *Introduction to Scientific Thought* (San Diego: Cognella, 2012).

revelation, Galileo said, "For the Holy Bible and the phenomena of nature proceed alike from the Divine Word, the former as the dictate of the Holy Spirit, and the latter as the observant executor of God's commands."[22] So far, so good for the relationship between Christian theism and science.

This cozy relationship between theism and science took a turn with the career of the Englishman Francis Bacon (no relation to Roger) and something like a U-turn with that of Isaac Newton. Francis Bacon (1561-1626) has been hyperbolically described as the father of modern science with his proposal of an empirical scientific method. He saw the sciences not so much as means to understanding the Creator but as a means to improve the human condition. As a humanist, he said that "knowledge ought to bear fruit in works, that science ought to apply to industry, that men ought to organize themselves as a sacred duty to improve and transform the conditions of life."[23] Bacon's vision proved to be prophetic. As moderns, or even as postmodernists, we do not argue with Bacon's vision that science can and should improve the human condition. Still, with Bacon, science became a servant of humanity and not principally a source of general revelation about a Creator.

Rene Descartes (1596-1650)

By the late seventeenth century, Western Europeans entered what is sometimes called the Age of Enlightenment or the Age of Reason. Rationalist philosopher and mathematician Rene Descartes (1596-1650) paved the way. He proposed that the human mind is the ultimate source of truth. He famously said, "I think, therefore I am." A dualist philosopher, he proposed that the human body and the mind are two completely separate entities, with the mind being over the body. Blaise Pascal, a contemporary of Descartes, decried his turn from theism, saying, "I cannot forgive Descartes; in all his philosophy, Descartes did his best to dispense with God. But Descartes could not avoid prodding God to set the world in motion with a snap of his lordly fingers; after that he had no use for God." Descartes did not publicly acknowledge what Pascal

---

22   Ibid.
23   Benjamin Farrington, Francis Bacon: *Philosopher of Industrial Science* (London: Octagon, 1979), p. 3.

saw him doing, which was to pave an exit ramp from Christian theism to deism.

With the career of Isaac Newton (1642-1727), the worldview we call deism came out into the open. We will discuss the deistic view of the world in a later chapter. Right now, we are primarily concerned with following the road from Christian theism to Christian deism to atheism. Isaac Newton was the greatest mathematician and scientist of his age, but his role as a theologian and philosopher is hardly less significant. He has been credited with being the father of the Enlightenment. The most significant contribution of Newton was his proposal of what he called the Mechanical Universe. According to Newton, the universe created by God is like a finely-tuned machine that God wound up and let go. Newton was not an atheist. He rhetorically asked, "Whence is it that nature does nothing in vain; and whence arises all the order and beauty which we see in the world?" To this question, Newton would have replied that the order and beauty we see in the world come from the One who created the universe—God. But Newton's God was, first and foremost, a Creator. Newton's God does not need to involve himself in working his beautiful machine. Newton, like other deists, did not believe that the Creator intervenes supernaturally in the world at all. He rejected the idea of miracles, including the resurrection of Christ. In Newton, we see science no longer as the means to know God. For some who came after the great Newton, science became a reason to deny the existence of a supernatural Creator altogether.

We will see below that the worldview known as deism is inherently unstable. This proved true historically in the eighteenth and nineteenth centuries. If God's only role is to wind up the universe and let it go, then why ought we to invoke God at all? Newton's deism, like that of French philosophes such as Voltaire, leaves little for God to do. It also radically undermines the idea of biblical inspiration. If God did not supernaturally part the Red Sea or raise Jesus of Nazareth from the dead, why would he intervene to produce an inspired book? Why not let the subject of truth be decided by human reasoning alone? These questions carried greater and greater weight in Western Europe in the Age of Enlightenment.

This leads us, inexorably, to atheism—to a thorough naturalism and a godless determinism. Historically, deism has been a slippery slope from theism to atheism. In the seventeenth century, Descartes was careful to conceal his skepticism. The only crucial literary figure in the seventeenth century to take off the gloves as a confirmed atheist was Thomas Hobbes (1588-1679), author of *Leviathan*. Hobbes was a materialist who said that humans are entirely material beings. According to Hobbes, God is a material being if he exists. Such reticence to come out as an atheist became unnecessary in eighteenth and nineteenth-century Europe. With the likes of the Scottish philosopher David Hume (1711-1776), we begin to see an open skepticism and even atheism. Even in the eighteenth century, Hume's open rejection of the idea of a Creator was rare, with most skeptics opting for deism.

Pierre-Simone Laplace (1749-1827)

Only in the nineteenth century did we begin to find small but significant numbers in Western Europe and the United States willing to avow atheism. The French Revolution produced several atheists. Among them is French polymath genius Pierre-Simone Laplace (1749-1827). He published a five-volume treatise, *Celestial Mechanics,* applying differential equations to expand on the work of Isaac Newton. He proposed a "causal determinism" whereby his mathematical physics could, in principle, use the laws of physics to allow present conditions to be extrapolated into the past or into the future. His universe was entirely mechanical and deterministic. In a famous interview with Napoleon, the emperor asked Laplace concerning his treatise, "Monsieur Laplace, they tell me you have written this large book on the system of the universe and have never even mentioned its Creator." To this, the naturalist Laplace replied, "I have no need of that hypothesis."[24]

To Laplace, we can add the likes of Thomas Huxley (1825-1895), known as "Darwin's bulldog," for his dogged defense of Darwin's theory of evolution. Darwin was reticent to declare his worldview openly, but the evidence points to his being a deist. However, his close friend and ally Huxley can be described as an atheist, although he coined the term agnostic and called himself one. And then there is Karl Marx (1818-1883), philosopher,

---

24   Some say that this story is semi-apocryphal, but more than one eye-witness to the event reported versions of the events which are similar.

creator of communism, and author of *The Communist Manifesto*. Marx provocatively said that "religion is the opiate of the people." Marxism has been described as its own unique worldview—one which views economics and the politics of power as the chief components of human reality. Marx's worldview has been called historical materialism, "an argument that the world is changed not by ideas but by actual, physical, material activity and practice." Friedrich Nietzsche (1844-1900) can be described as an atheist (he did, after all, famously declare that "God is dead, he remains dead, and we killed him."[25]). He flirted with nihilism. This is the worldview that nothing is important and that life completely lacks purpose and meaning. He also laid the philosophical groundwork for 20th-century postmodernism, with its radical rejection of coherent objective truth in favor of his "perspectivism." His idea of the *Ubermensch* (literally

Friedrich Nietzsche (1844-1900)

over-man) was hijacked by the Nazis and their cynical national socialism. Influential 20th-century materialists include Vladimir Lenin, Bertrand Russel, Isaac Asimov, Richard Dawkins, and Steven Hawking.

We are about to analyze whether scientific materialism is a "good" worldview, but let us summarize our brief history. Before the nineteenth century, naturalism—the idea that only material things are real—was rare. Historically it developed from a conjunction between Isaac Newton's scientific idea of the Mechanical Universe and the secular humanist idea that human reason is the ultimate decider of what is true and what is real. Is this a good worldview? Well, it certainly is depressing, but if it were true, perhaps we should embrace it anyway. To this, the first question, we now turn to.

Is It True?

Our first measure of the goodness of a worldview is whether it is true. By this, we mean to ask whether the presuppositions of materialism are

---

25   Friedrich Nietzsche, "The Madman." *Gay Science* 125 in *The Portable Nietzsche,* trans. Walter Kaufman (New York: Viking, 1954), p. 95-96.

consistent with what we know about reality. The simple answer to this question is no. Scientific materialism is not valid. It is a false perspective for several reasons, among which are the following. Naturalism is wrong because:

It is based on circular reasoning.

The universe was created.

Life was created.

One reason I conclude that naturalism is not true is that those who deny the reality of the supernatural inevitably resort to circular reasoning to defend their belief. How do I know that only material things are real? Because I assume that only material things are real. No one says this, but in practice, this is how naturalist reasoning works. Of course, if one defending a particular belief puts up a weak argument, this does not prove that the view is untrue. Still, if nearly all supporting an idea, including those who are well-prepared, use the same weak argument, this makes us suspicious that the belief is not true.

To illustrate, recently, I was listening to the audio from a BBC broadcast.[26] The show's premise was that a panel of academic scholars would question experts on either side of a debate. In this case, the question was about the existence of God. The materialist in the docket was a well-known scientist. He was asked to give an opening statement. In doing so, he declared with great confidence that the only things which are real are things which can be observed and measured using the scientific method. All other things are simply not real. This is the classic naturalist view of the world. The first panelist to cross-examine the professor asked him a simple question. "You say that only observable, physical entities are real. How do you know that?" In other words, do you have any evidence to support your principal conclusion? The atheist gentleman responded with a rant against organized religions—especially fundamentalists of all varieties. The panelist pointed out that this was not an answer to his question. "Please, sir, answer the question. How do you know that only material things are real?" To this, the determinist responded with a second rant against the terrible things done in the name of religion (some of which are probably true, but...). The panelist interrupted the rant. "Excuse me, sir,

26 I have not yet found the original episode. This account is a rather loose paraphrase of the actual event.

but you need to answer the question. Otherwise, we will ask you to step down." The now-less-confident naturalist hesitated for a moment before replying. "I guess I just believe it to be true."

There you go. This is circular reasoning. I have often heard materialists claim with similar confidence that science has disproved the reality of miracles and the supernatural. This claim is utter nonsense, and one would think that materialists would be aware of the circular reasoning being used. Science, by definition, only deals with natural things. The realm of inquiry of the scientific method is things that are both observable and reproducible. By their very nature, if miracles happen, such miracles would be supernatural—they would break the laws of nature. It has been said that the only way to disprove the reality of the supernal would be to have a supernal perspective. Or, as Michael Aeschliman put it, "Any theory that denies the transcendence of the theorist is self-refuting."[27] One would think that most naturalists would be sufficiently self-aware to recognize their belief that only material things are real is simply that—a belief. It is an unfounded presupposition. One would be wrong.

Another illustration comes from a debate that an organization I am president of put on a few years ago.[28] The premise was *"Does God Exist?"* My good friend Douglas Jacoby defended quite well the premise that God exists. Some of his arguments will be presented when we analyze the theistic worldview. Essential for us to hear are the opinions his opponent, Michael Shermer, used. Shermer is a science writer, the president of The Skeptics Society, and the founding editor of the *Skeptic* magazine (and, by the way, a friend and a nice guy). Shermer, an experienced debater, avoided many easily-refuted arguments for atheism, such as the fact that we cannot "see" God or the non sequitur argument that so much evil has been done in the name of God. Believe it or not, his only actual argument, other than a few quips and catchy sayings, was that atheism is the default argument. In other words, unless you can prove that God is real, then the logical conclusion is that he is not real, even if we have no evidence that he does not exist. According to whom is atheism the default argument, especially given that the vast majority of well-educated folks have believed in the supernatural? Why does Shermer believe that only material things

---

27 Michael D. Aeschliman, *The Restitution of Man* (Grand Rapids, MI: Eerdmans, 1983), p. ix.
28 The debate is available on video from www.ipibooks.com.

are real? Because he believes that only material things are real. That is not a good argument.

The second reason I conclude with great confidence that materialism is not true is the apparent fact that the universe was created. Until the mid-twentieth century, the consensus cosmological model of scientists was that the universe is eternal and, therefore, uncreated. Did they have empirical evidence to support this presupposition? No, they (or perhaps I should say "we" because I am a scientist) did not. This was the accepted view, more for philosophical than scientific reasons. Why? Because if the universe was created, then this has philosophical implications which are troubling to the materialist.

I do not have the space here to give a thorough treatment of the history of the big bang model, but suffice it to say that from evidence proving the expanding universe, from the cosmic background microwave radiation, and from the distribution of the original elements in the universe, the consensus cosmological model today is known colloquially as the big bang. The nearly universally accepted cosmology is this: Roughly 13.5 billion years ago, a "singularity" occurred, from which the entire known universe emerged. Before this event, there was no matter, no energy—in fact, there was not even space or time itself. There was, quite literally, nothing before the big bang. Science being what it is, the big bang cannot be proved, but all the evidence is consistent with the conclusion that the universe—something—was created from nothing.

This brings us back to one of those questions that science is not very good at answering: Why? Why does anything exist at all? If the universe has a beginning, what or who created it? If you have an atheist friend, you may want to ask her or him this question. It seems common sense that a created universe has a Creator. Whether that "Creator" is a person or not is an open question, but the evidence says that something came from nothing. This implies a supernal, non-physical Creator of some sort.

William Lane Craig has proposed a version of the Cosmological Argument known as the Kalam Cosmological argument. It goes like this:

Premise: Anything that begins to exist was caused.

Premise: The universe began to exist.

Conclusion: The universe was caused, and that cause is the Creator.

David Hume denied the reality of cause and effect, but he remains alone on this. He is an outlier. He did not have an actual example to provide to us of an uncaused effect. His argument was a philosophical/logical one, not based on reality. Common sense and experience tell us that the first premise above is true. Things that begin to exist are caused, without exception. We know that the universe began to exist as surely as we know anything from science. If the first two premises are true, then scientific materialism is untrue—end of the story.

A third argument that materialism is patently false is found in the existence of life. There are two things all of us can agree on. The universe exists, and life exists. Does the reality of life prove a Creator of that life? My answer, as a Ph.D. chemist and physicist, is a resounding yes! Let us see why.

In 1859 Louis Pasteur, who devised the germ theory, did a series of experiments in which he disproved what had been called the theory of spontaneous generation. Before these conclusive experiments, some scientists had believed that elementary life forms, such as bacteria, can be spontaneously generated from non-living substances, life from non-life. In these experiments, Pasteur conclusively demonstrated that "life comes only from life." If true, then that is the end of the story. If Spontaneous generation, otherwise known as abiogenesis, is proven false, then life was supernaturally created. Materialism is proved wrong again.

Louis Pasteur (1822-1895)

Not so fast. Pasteur demonstrated in his experiments that life is not currently spontaneously generated. The accepted fact is that life exists, and the question is not whether it is being spontaneously generated today. The question is whether it is reasonable to believe that in the deep past, a single event occurring on a planet with an environment vastly different from that on the earth today might have produced a single living thing from a non-living chemical soup. If so, all life could have descended from this original spontaneously created cell. If such a proposed "soup" of organic matter were to exist on the current earth, bacteria would almost immediately eat the soup, ending any spontaneous generation experiment. Such would not be the case in an ancient theoretical world.

For this reason, Pasteur's experiments are irrelevant to the question of the origin of life. However, we are left with the question of abiogenesis. Let it be noted that atheists are strongly predisposed to believe in abiogenesis. If they are wrong on this, they are wrong in their entire worldview! Circular reasoning is a significant factor here. What would be required for life to arise from non-life? The answer to this question is complex, and it involves a lot of biochemistry which is beyond the scope of our basic analysis here. It is dealt with thoroughly in my book, *Is There a God?*[29] To simplify, a spontaneously created living thing would have to be composed of an almost unimaginably complex but accidental mixture of lipids (fats), polysaccharides (sugars), proteins (polymers of amino acids) and nucleic acids (polymers of nucleotides). Primitive environments have been proposed which can produce a random mixture of amino acids but not functional proteins. Different primitive environments have been presented which would spontaneously make nucleotides but not functional DNA or RNA. Still, other environments have been proposed which can produce simple lipids, but this environment does not produce amino acids or nucleotides—the same for polysaccharides.

Add to these sseemingly insurmountable problems for abiogenesis is the greatest difficulty of all. If there is any idea in science that approaches the level of fact, it is the laws of thermodynamics. The second law of thermodynamics allows us to predict what we already know from experiments, which is that nature does not ever produce information without the input of pre-existent information. The insurmountable problem for any theory of abiogenesis is that the simplest living thing requires a great deal of information. Millions of pieces of such information are found in even the most simple life. To propose that life came from non-life, one must propose a process similar to a million letters being thrown into the air and falling to the earth to produce a sensible, readable book. Such a process is simply impossible, and invoking a great length of time does not solve this problem.

The impossibility of abiogenesis is more profound even than this.

29   John Oakes, *Is There a God? Questions* (Spring, TX: IPI Books, 2006). I also suggest a more thorough discussion of abiogenesis by Stephen C. Meyer, *Signature in the Cell* (New York: HarperCollins, 2009).

This is because proteins are only created by DNA, and DNA is only created by proteins. Therefore, the simplest life would have to contain the DNA, which would have created the protein (but it did not) in the same place as the protein which would have created the DNA (except that it was not)! This is like the question of which came first, the chicken or the egg. It is the chicken and the egg problem on steroids. Which came first, the DNA or the protein? The answer from materialists is that they were created at the same time and in the same place, both by a long series of singularly beneficial accidents. Can anyone believe this? The answer is that no reasonable person could believe this. Yet some do. They do so because of presuppositional arguments and by circular reasoning, not because it is reasonable.

There are several other reasons we can be confident that naturalism is false. For example, if materialism is true, there is no moral imperative, and rape is not wrong. But all of us know that rape is just plain wrong. If determinism is true, then there is no inherent design in nature, but all of us know that there is a great deal of design in nature. Other arguments can be enumerated, all of which disprove atheist assumptions. The materialist worldview is just plain not true. Scientific materialism is invalid, and this is sufficient reason to reject this worldview. That being said, it is time to move to our second criterion for whether a worldview is good.

Is It Right?

The atheist worldview is false. Next, we will ask if it is right. Be reminded that by this, we are asking whether it gives satisfactory and believable answers to the questions people care about. How did I get here? Where am I going? What, if any, are my purpose and my value? What is the right thing to do? The determinist worldview does a terrible job of answering these questions.

How did I get here and why am I here? If we take the word of Julian Huxley, quoted above, we got here by "a singular series of beneficial accidents." We are the result of a sheer accident of nature. If this is true, it is pretty depressing, but is it even true? Some sad things are nevertheless true. Can any human being look at the surpassingly complex physical, psychological, moral, and spiritual things we know of as human beings and believe that we are the product of random collisions between molecules and biological accidents? Really? This is not a good answer to the essential question of why I am here.

Who am I? The very question assumes that "I" exist. But in materialism is a correct worldview, then "I" do not exist. For example, I say, "I want to go to the store." If determinism is correct, then I deceive myself, both by using the word "I" and by using the word "want," because if the materialist is right, then human consciousness is merely an epiphenomenon. What am I? If the scientific materialist is correct, "I" am simply a sack of chemicals and cells that does what it does because nerve cells are firing in particular ways determined by a series of previous chemical reactions caused by sensory impressions interacting with DNA-generated chemicals. "I" am an epiphenomenon, and when I say I "want" something, what does that even mean? My chemicals and neural networks are making me believe that I want that thing, but this wanting is just the result of neurotransmitters being released and neurons firing in a particular way. Again, can any rational person agree with this premise? Naturalism does a poor job of answering the question of who I am.

Then there is the question of value. What is my value, my worth? If the materialist is correct, my value is a few dollars, as I am made up of some carbon, some nitrogen, some sodium, potassium, iodine, iron, manganese, and small amounts of other precious metals. Naturalism is quite ineffective at establishing the value of things. To the scientist, iron is more valuable than gold, and elm trees are more valuable than humans because both iron and elm trees can be used to build things. I have no actual inherent value at all! Again, atheism is falling far short here. We will see the superiority of the Christian worldview on this question.

What is my purpose? Let us ask the believing materialist. Do I have a purpose? Maybe. If so, my purpose is to create as many copies of my DNA as possible. Think about this for a moment. If the "purpose" of human life is to create many copies of my DNA, this is an alarming thought. What actions might be justified if I understand that my donation to progress in the universe is to create many copies of my presumably superior DNA? We will see that on the questions of value and purpose, Christian theism does infinitely better here. But maybe the materialist is right. Perhaps the minority opinion that humans have a purposeless life is true. Is our belief in purpose and meaning due to wishful thinking? Let the reader decide.

Next is the question of what is the right thing to do. Naturalism is not helpful here in the least. In a materialist world, morality is undefined. If I am the product of a long series of singularly beneficial accidents, then there is no moral truth. If determinism is true, then words like justice and rights are meaningless. There is no justice, and there is no right and wrong. Any kind of sexual behavior is equally right or wrong as any other. Who is to say that murder is wrong? In a materialist world, murder may be unethical, but it is not immoral because morality, by its very definition, is a matter of absolutes, but materialism rejects the idea of moral absolutes. Determinism cannot establish such moral absolutes. Random meaningless events do not lead to morality.

Here is how C. S. Lewis put it:

> "If an accidental collision brought about the solar system, then the appearance of organic life on this planet was also an accident, and the whole evolution of Man was an accident too. If so, then all our thought processes are mere accidents—the accidental by-product of the movement of atoms. And this holds for the materialists' and astronomers' as well as for anyone else's [thought processes]. But if their thoughts—i.e., of Materialism and Astronomy—are merely accidental by-products, why should we believe them to be true? I see no reason for believing that one accident would be able to give a correct account of all the other accidents."[30]

Where do I go after my death? To this question, naturalists have an unambiguous answer. When we die, we cease to exist. We change from something to nothing. When we are dead, we are dead like Rover, dead all over. Atheism gives confusing answers to other important questions, but on this question, there is no confusion to the determinist. If the

C.S. Lewis (1898-1963)

materialist is correct, then human beings should accept this reality rather than turn to all the wishful thinking found in pantheism, polytheism, and theism. But is death the end of existence? Maybe so, but one thing to remember is that in the preceding section, we already showed that atheism is not true. If materialism is not true, ought we to trust its answer to the question of life after death? A great majority of humans who have ever

---

30 C. S. Lewis, *God in the Dock* (Grand Rapids, MI: Eerdmans, 1970), p. 52-53.

lived have rejected this answer, but the majority does not determine what is true. Do theists have proof of life after death or do pantheists have evidence of reincarnation? This is something to be thought about long and hard.

If materialism is our worldview, then love is also a nonsense word. "Love" is a certain pattern of neurons associated with the release of certain neurotransmitters caused by external events. If naturalism is correct, then I cannot "love" someone. Love is merely an epiphenomenon. But all of us know that love is real. Again, scientific materialism falls utterly flat in addressing every single one of the questions people care so deeply about. If materialism is true, then all religious ideas are pure nonsense, and when I pray, I am talking to myself (except that "I" do not exist). Then beauty is just a mathematical concept, and human history is meaningless.

If you spend enough time talking to your atheist friends, they will soon reveal that they do not believe in their worldview, at least not completely (of course, to some extent, this can be said of Christian theists as well). You tell them that your country ought to be run by Christian ideals. "That is wrong," they reply. But according to their worldview, there is no right and wrong. If you throw an atheist in prison for espousing their worldview, they will proclaim that their rights are being violated. I agree, but I believe in "rights" because I also believe in human dignity. What is the basis for the concept of human rights in a materialist world?

Is It Better?

We now turn to our third criterion for whether scientific materialism is a "good" worldview. Is it a better set of presuppositions than the alternative proposed worldviews? Would a reasonable person with an unbiased perspective agree that a person who is a true materialist would be motivated by that materialism to be the best possible person? Remember the qualities we are looking for. Would the natural result of believing that only material things are real tend to produce a person who is humble, generous, courageous, diligent, self-controlled, honest, self-sacrificing, compassionate, and peace-loving?

Let me immediately jump in to defend my atheist friends. I have a lot of such friends because I am a scientist, and I have worked among scientists for my entire professional life. Those who claim that almost all scientists are either agnostic or atheist are wrong. Multiple studies have proved this. For example, a Pew Research study in 2009 revealed that, among practicing scientists in that particular study, 33% believed in God (were theists), 18 % believed in some universal spirit or higher power (and were therefore probably pantheists), and 41% did not believe in either (and were most likely materialists or agnostics).[31] Despite the disparity between what most people believe about atheism among scientists, I swim in a sea largely populated by atheists, and my experience is that these materialist scientists are the ones who speak most loudly.

But let me tell you about my friend Dick Albert, with whom I co-taught the course *Intro to Scientific Thought* mentioned above. When we began working together, Dick was an atheist. We enjoyed staging mock debates in front of students in which I would take his view, and he would defend mine. My point is that Dr. Albert was one of the nicest, most respectful, humble, honest, diligent, and compassionate people I have known. By the way, after several years of talking about science and religion, my friend converted to deism. He said to me one day, "John, there is a Creator!" My personal experience with atheists is that, on average, they pay as much or even more attention to behaving ethically than the run-of-the-mill theist with whom I regularly interact. Maybe this is because most atheists I have known come from highly educated, privileged backgrounds. Or perhaps this is because they are sensitive to putting a good foot forward. Let us who are theists be careful against unfairly generalizing about those who hold other views of the world.

The question, though, is this. If we consider materialism to be the source of this "good" behavior, is it logically consistent? My answer is no, and I explain the relatively good behavior of many materialists by my observation that their concept of what is good and ethical is hijacked mainly from the Christian worldview. I will argue below that the Western world rejected slavery because of Christian theism, that they developed science out of a Christian worldview, and that the idea of human dignity and human rights evolved out of a world that received its basic set of presuppositions from Christianity. If we removed what our culture received from its Christian foundation, what would a world which evolved from a materialist perspective look like? This is the question.

---

31 https://www.pewresearch.org/religion/2009/11/05/scientists-and-belief/ By the way, in the same survey of Americans generally, conducted in 2006, only 4% classified themselves as non-believers. Perhaps most interestingly, whereas 18% of the scientists appear to have a pantheistic worldview, only 13% of the general population have such a worldview, while 83% believed in God.

This would be a world in which there is no basis for making purely moral decisions. It would be a world in which lying might be a bad idea (because it is unethical), but it would not be wrong. It would be a world in which there is no natural basis for assuming that "all people were created equal." In fact, in this world, eugenics (the selection of who will be born based on better or worse genes) makes a lot of sense. It would be a world in which human beings have no inherent value or purpose for living. It would be a world in which the word justice, if it has any meaning at all, could be only arbitrarily defined. It would be a world where survival of the fittest may be an essential ethic. It would be a world in which dogs might be justified in eating dogs, as they say. This is a world in which violence, genocide, and hatred are neither inherently good nor evil.

Do we want to live in a world molded by such presuppositions? By the way, the experiment has been tried. We have had a limited number of human experiments in the past in which materialist assumptions were allowed to run rampant. This includes the experiments of the Soviet Union, Red China, and the French Revolution. These avowedly atheistic experiments (or perhaps deistic in the case of France after 1789) did not turn out very well. We can learn from these disasters. Have theists done a consistently great job of being "good"? Clearly not, and let us not pretend differently. However, when a Christian theist does evil, at least there is, in principle, a moral absolute found in their worldview, which informs us that the action is evil. In a purely materialist society, evil is not clear. It is not even defined.

As we complete our analysis of whether naturalism is a good worldview, remember that in modern, Western societies, so much of what we have received as good, we acquired from Christian theism. The things we value so much are being hijacked from a worldview receding over time. As Michael Aeschliman said, "Science is a good servant but a bad master."[32] Do we, as a people, want to live in a world in which materialist presuppositions determine how we live? This is something for us to think carefully about.

32　Michael D. Aeschliman, *The Restitution of Man* (Grand Rapids, MI: Eerdmans, 1983), p. ix.

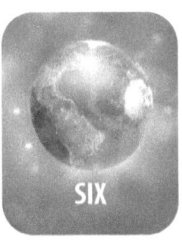

SIX

Postmodernism

The second worldview we will be describing and analyzing is postmodernism. This will be our most challenging task because postmodernism is the worldview which holds that no single legitimate worldview exists. It is the worldview-less worldview. The postmodern rejects the very idea of objective truth, which will make our analysis of whether postmodernism is true problematic. If we ask a postmodernist what is true, he or she will tell us that nothing is absolutely true. Either that or they will say that truth is what you believe it to be. "It is true for you, but not for me." Postmodernism leaves behind absolutes and states that all truth is relative. It seems to violate common sense. This can be very frustrating.

I will use a personal incident in my life to illustrate where postmodernism is taking us. I was speaking at Stockholm University just over a decade ago. This was at a time when I was just beginning to understand where the postmodern mind is taking us. I was giving a presentation on why I believe in God. One of my arguments for the reality of God I used that night was the moral argument. I made what I thought was an obvious and common-sense statement: "Some things are just plain wrong, whether we believe them to be or not." A woman at the presentation reacted extremely negatively to my saying this. In fact, she nearly fell out of her seat. When I talked to her after the presentation she appeared to be shaken. She was having trouble breathing. To her, it was virtually unimaginable that anyone would have the nerve certain things—certain moral statements—are just plain true and that those who disagree are therefore wrong. In her radical postmodern world, the only real sin was to call anything sinful. This event was a wake-up call to me of where postmodernism is taking our culture.

The dominant worldview in universities in the Western world today is not materialism. In fact, outside of those who inhabit the hard sciences, the materialist/modernist worldview has mainly been left behind and replaced by a postmodern worldview in academia. Interestingly, when I talk to my fellow professors on the other side of the campus (where the softer sciences are taught), many of them scoff at postmodernism as a philosophy but appear to me to be thoroughly postmodern in their perspective. In the last forty years, postmodernism left the academy and entered our culture in force. We have entered the postmodern age. In the West, we now swim in a principally postmodern sea. It is difficult to describe to outsiders, or even ourselves, what the postmodern take on reality and culture is, as we need a balcony view of ourselves. What is the postmodern worldview, what is its history, and is it a "good" perspective on reality? To these questions, we now turn.

In the previous chapter, we allowed the intellectual history of the West to help us explain the genesis of naturalism and even to understand what the materialist worldview is. To understand the postmodern explanation of truth, it will be even more important to trace the history of this intellectual, artistic, and cultural perspective. We will trace the path from the pre-modern age to the modern era to the postmodern age. In doing so, we will do something that postmodernists prefer we avoid doing: looking at history through an entirely Western perspective because the pre-modern, the modern, and the postmodern view developed in the West.

The pre-modern Western world was a God-centered world. The source of authority and truth before Galileo, Newton, and Descartes was the Bible (or perhaps the Church and its tradition if you were an Orthodox or a Catholic believer). The pre-modern moved from being to knowing. Anselm of Canterbury said, "I believe in order to know." What I know is determined by who or whose I am. The individual's importance was relative to the Christian community in which they lived.

With Descartes and Newton in the seventeenth and early eighteenth centuries, the West entered the modern era. Descartes told us that we move from knowing to becoming. "I think, therefore I am." The West passed from a perspective that the truth is delivered to us from God to the idea that human reasoning is the gauge of what is true. For many, this caused a shift from theism to deism, and for some, even the change to a godless naturalism. But we must be aware that Christianity was very much involved in the modern Enlightenment experiment. The modernist church stressed the right of the individual to interpret the Bible for themselves, and Americanized Christianity moved from a pre-modern community-centered to a modern individual-centered focus.

The modernist, whether theist, deist, or atheist, had a optimistic view of the human predicament. Applying our innate ability to reason allowed us to become better and better. In the human-centered modern world, humans were improving over time. The secular humanist was convinced that humanity would ultimately overcome our failures and limitations. Nineteenth-century Christian eschatology was postmillennial. We were about to enter the Christian age in which the gospel truth would prevail.

The reason that modernity gave way to postmodernism is, of course, complex, but we will look at three factors. The first is the scientific paradigm shift from Newtonian classical physics to modern physics. The second is a series of world events that destroyed Europeans' confidence in the goodness and reasonableness of human beings. The third is the entropy-inducing philosophy of Friedrich Nietzsche.

Newton and successors such as Laplace had described a classical physics which was well-described by mathematics and which was deterministic. As discussed earlier, Laplace claimed that with a set of exact initial conditions, he could use differential equations to determine both the past and the future. In classical physics particles were particles and waves were waves. Beginning in 1905, Albert Einstein and others completely upended classical mechanics. With the discovery of the quantum model, scientists came to understand that the past does not determine the future. There is an element of uncertainty, and the future is a matter of probability—it is not certain. Also, Einstein showed that light is neither wholly described as a wave nor a particle, and his successors proved that what we thought were particles, such as electrons, was acting like waves. Assumed categories were demolished by quantum mechanics. When Einstein published his special and general theories of relativity, even space, time, and mass were no longer well distinguished and their values were shown to be relative to motion. These two paradigm-shattering discoveries caused naturalists to question their basic assumptions about how human reason can lead to definite knowledge about the universe.

This, however, mainly affected only intellectuals at the time. The second factor may be the principal cause of the end of the age of Reason. The twin apocalyptic tragedies of World Wars I and II, including the horrors of Auschwitz and the German "final solution, culminating in the terrifying events at Hiroshima and Nagasaki, had the result of obliterating optimism about the essential goodness of human beings and their ability to grow and learn through the use of human reasoning. The idea of human progress was shattered. The Enlightenment ideal of applying human reason to discover a central truth about the universe was disintegrating.

The third harbinger of postmodernism preceded modern physics and the two world wars. The philosophical work of Friedrich Nietzsche anticipated by almost eighty years the breakdown of modernism. Nietzsche has been called the "patron saint of postmodern philosophy." Nietzsche was a troubled soul from his youth. Yet, he was an acknowledged genius at a very young age, attaining a full professorship in philology at the University of Basel at the age of twenty-four. He soon began to question the foundational philosophical underpinnings of Western thought. The modernist sought to use human reasoning to obtain the truth about the universe. Nietzsche questioned the very existence of truth itself. He described truth as "a mobile army of metaphors." He called truth "an illusion" and "a worn-out metaphor without power." Nietzsche claimed that truth depends on language. He said that truth is created, not discovered by humans. It took eighty years and two world wars for Nietzsche's ideas to be accepted more broadly by philosophers and the academic world. Still, it eventually led to radical relativism, producing a new worldview.

James Sire beautifully summarizes the transition from the pre-modern to the modern to the postmodern. It is "....a movement from the Christian premodern notion of revealed determinate metanarrative to the modern notion of the autonomy of human reason with access to the truth of correspondence to the postmodern notion that we create truth as we construct languages that serve our purposes."[33] I have not yet defined the word metanarrative. It is an important one in the discussion of postmodernism. A metanarrative is much like a worldview. It is "an overarching account or interpretation of events and circumstances that provide a pattern or structure for people's beliefs and gives meaning to their experiences."[34] A goal of postmodernism is to destroy all metanarratives (such as that in the Bible, for example). Jean-Francois Lyotard has described postmodernism as "incredulity toward metanarratives." There is no single true story or worldview. The following chart compares the three ways of knowing.

---

33 James W. Sire, *The Universe Next Door* (Downer's Grove II: Intervarsity Press, 2011), p. 213.
34 From Wikipedia.
35 Jean-Francois Lyotard, "The Postmodern Condition:" *A Report on Knowledge,* trans. Geoff Bennington and Brian Massumi (Minneapolis: University of Minnesota Press, 1984), p. 24.

The seismic shift

PREMODERN	MODERN	POST-MODERN
Belief in Divinity	Ambivalent about divinity	Divinity is Self-Expression
Conviction is a virtue Tolerance is evil	Rationality is a virtue	Tolerance is a virtue Conviction is bad
Authority is God	Authority is logic and science	Authority is self or or the group
Change brought about by adherence to a standard	Change brought about by what is rational	Change contingent on self-expression & culture

By the 1960s and 1970s, philosophers such as Michael Foucault (said, "Truth is a fabrication." and "The act of knowing is always an act of violence."), Jacques Derrida (said, "Reading is a violent act of mastery over the text." Invented deconstruction of metanarrative), and Richard Rorty ("said Truth is found in coherence, not correspondence") began to have significant influence in academic circles. Historians of science also got on the bandwagon with the influential work of Thomas Kuhn (1922-1996). Kuhn argued that science does not progress by a Baconian "scientific method," in which science uses inductive and deductive processes to produce theories consistent with experimental evidence.[36] Instead, he claimed that the process of research, and the theories which are proposed are determined by a scientific paradigm—a guiding cultural presupposition. As Karl Popper put it, "scientific observation is theory-laden." Kuhn said that a scientific paradigm is a social construction of reality. The reader may be surprised to know that the history of science has tended to confirm rather than disprove the influence of scientific culture on scientific discovery.

If postmodern thinking had remained constrained to the halls of academia, we would not be talking about this worldview here. By the 1980s, a ripple of postmodern thinking was felt in the broader culture, and by the 1990s, this ripple became a tidal wave. In the twenty-first century, we

---

36 For example, Thomas Kuhn, *The Structure of Scientific Revolutions* (Chicago: University of Chicago Press, 1962)

can see the effects of postmodern thinking in every aspect of culture, art, and, yes, even religion. Before we look at some of these effects, let us be reminded of the presuppositions of postmodernism.

In postmodernism, overarching metanarratives are rejected. Truth is truly relative to those who hold to it. All stories are equally valued. Postmodernism is the storyless story, or it is the story of many equally valuable (and therefore valueless) stories. We can have meaning, but we cannot have the truth. We can ask whether a statement is useful but not whether it is true. The postmodern world is a centerless world. The theories we devise create the different worlds we inhabit, none of which are more valid than any other. The only truth is that there is no truth. This lack of a center can be very unsettling for some and very freeing for others.

The effects of this worldview are many. The postmodern values diversity over unity. Most of us would agree that tolerance is a good human quality, but the postmodernist raises tolerance to the highest possible level of good. To tell someone that they are wrong, even on what may seem rather obviously untrue statements, is to commit the ultimate cultural sin, which is to be intolerant. The postmodern is inherently eclectic. Music fusion, a fusion of culinary styles, a fusion of Eastern with Western philosophy and religion, every possible kind of fusion, is valued in a postmodern world. People say, "Act locally, think globally." The result on music and food is positive, but the erosion of truth and metanarrative is something that needs to be evaluated.

Fifty years ago in the United States, there were three television networks. On any night, as much as one-third of all eyes saw the same program. When a song rose to the top of the pop music charts, almost everyone was singing the same song, and this included the Western world more broadly. Given the rise of postmodern thinking, it is not an accident that there are dozens of entertainment outlets and hundreds of channels. The music scene is so fractured that only a small minority of any age group listens to any particular style of music. This centrifugal micro-fracturing of culture results from the rise of the valueless worldview we call postmodernism. Its effect on music, art, and literature may be a good thing, but what about its effect on the human psyche, the idea of morality, and the violent assault on the idea of authority and propositional truth? A generation ago, there were two genders, and the vast majority were quite clear about what their gender was. Now, it is hard to count the number and kinds of genders, and many, especially the young, are still determining where they will land. Whether this is a good or a bad thing is something to be discussed, but one thing we can be sure of. This fracturing of the concept of gender is the result of a postmodern mindset and worldview.

We are about to embark on our worldview analysis of postmodernism, but before we do, let us consider the effect of postmodernism on religious thinking. It is ironic that postmodernism, which proposes that all truth is relative to culture, has had a significant impact on those who hold to alternative worldviews. In other words, one can be a theist, a pantheist, or a materialist and be a postmodernist, and we can range from 90% of one and 10% of the other to 10% of one and 90% of the other. Naturalism and postmodernism can be kissing cousins. To a lesser extent, even pantheism, with its relatively eclectic and flexible canon of scripture, can have a somewhat cozy relationship with postmodern ideas, but what about Christian or Islamic theism, with their heavy reliance on authoritative Scripture as a source of propositional truths? Islam and pre-modern Christian traditions such as Orthodox and Roman Christianity will be able to hold out as an island in a postmodern world, but what about modernist-influenced Protestant, Pentecostal, and Evangelical Christianity?

We can already see postmodern thinking heavily influencing schools of theology in the Christian world in the past 20 years. In churches influenced by modernism, doctrine is highly valued, and acceptance of propositional truths is key to salvation. This idea is rapidly disappearing. Many theologians today tell us that the Bible does not include propositional truth statements at all—that the Bible is, first and foremost, a narrative about God. Of course, there is truth here. In fact, postmodernism has made a positive contribution in that it has helped to transform an overly Westernized, hyper-individualized Christianity, which is excessively indebted to a rational description of an esoteric, communal core of Christianity. Modernism tells us that Christianity must be rational. Yet ideas such as trinity and substitutional atonement, though not irrational, are also not strictly rational. Postmodernism helps to accept this reality. Modernism rejects mystery, but postmodernism embraces mystery, as does the Bible. Postmodernism is not all bad for theism. However, in a world governed by postmodern thinking, those who hold to a theistic worldview may find some of the bedrock they have stood on for hundreds of years turn from granite to jello in very rapid order, potentially bringing in chaos and even disintegration to a scripture-based, truth-based belief system.

Is Postmodernism True?

Are the presuppositions of the Postmodern worldview true? The answer is straightforward. No, they are not! Is it true that nothing is absolutely true in the common-sense meaning of the word true? No, it is not true. Postmodernism is self-refuting. Is it absolutely true that "nothing is absolutely true?" The postmodernist does not have a good answer to this question. I made the charge earlier that those who defend materialism inevitably resort to circular reasoning. With postmodernism, we are not talking about circular reasoning. It is not even reasoning at all. The postmodern description of reality is irrational. We can appreciate some of the contributions of the postmodern perspective to our understanding of culture and history, but to hold to this as a foundational worldview is a little like taking part in a circular firing squad. If nothing is true, then postmodernism is not true. By the way, this is why you will no longer find postmodernists in university philosophy departments. Postmodernism is incoherent philosophy, but philosophers seek coherence. Postmodern philosophers have split the scene. The irony is that they have left behind a world outside of philosophy, which has accepted this worldview to a great extent. But does it have defendable truth claims?

With the likes of Karl Popper and Thomas Kuhn, the early and idealistic assumption that science is a Baconian, linear, rational, unbiased means to acquire truth about the universe has been successfully undermined, and for good reason. However, surely science is onto something. The fact that scientific knowledge undeniably progresses must tell us something. Scientific knowledge is moving in a definite and irreversible direction. If it is not moving toward true things, what is it moving toward? Science tells us that gravity is real. The law of gravity would not be true for them, even if the postmodern is correct, then if enough people gather together, they can construct a society whose truth denies the reality of gravity. It would not be true for them, even if it is true for me. And it would be insulting and intolerant for me to point this out. This would not change the fact that gravity exists, and the members of this gravity-denying society will not be stepping off tenth-floor balconies. Otherwise, their belief system will disappear very quickly.

Relativity is a paradigm which replaced an earlier, falsified scientific paradigm we call classical mechanics. Are the two equally true, as postmodernism proposes? No. The relativity paradigm predicts that clocks will run more slowly as they move faster through space. When tested, this proves true and classical mechanics is proved false. An atomic clock was carried on a NASA space shuttle flight in the 1990s, and the clock got behind earth-bound atomic clocks in the precise amount predicted by the theory. Does this not imply that the idea is, at least in some sense, true? And would not theories that predict different behavior be refuted? Science is onto something, and certain propositions are true even if not proven absolutely. All scientific conclusions are tentative, and science cannot confirm its theories to be true. Science is an imperfect instrument, but the fact that science cannot "prove" the first law of thermodynamics does not mean that it is not either 1. absolutely true or 2. not absolutely true. It cannot be both, and therefore, postmodernism is not true.

I will accept that reason does not give reliable access to propositionally true things. Our senses deceive us at times, and our minds do as well. Philosophical postmodernism has helped me to understand this. It has also pointed out the fallacy of the modernist assumption that human reason is absolute. However, I cannot get away from some obviously true things that postmodernism says are not absolutely true. Either God exists, or he does not. Either the universe was created, or it is eternal. Let us assume the former for the moment. If God does exist, either he created the universe or he is coextensive with the universe. Either one of these two propositions is true, or possibly neither of them is true, but they are not both true. To say both are true is to speak utter nonsense. Again, postmodernism is emphatically not true. It is a false and even deceptive means of viewing reality.

Is Postmodernism Right?

Postmodernism is demonstrably false. If one wants to say it is a good worldview, this is a big problem. But, even though it is simply not true, perhaps it can provide helpful answers for us to the questions people want answered—questions such as where we come from, why we exist, what is our purpose, what is the nature of ultimate reality, what is our ultimate fate, and why are there suffering and evil in the world? If postmodernism is, technically, not "true," perhaps it has so much to offer us in answering life's most essential questions that we can settle for a nuanced relationship with this worldview. Maybe we can "eat the fish and spit out the bones" of postmodernism.

What is my value? Some say that we are merely a random collection of atoms, molecules, cells, and tissues—the result of a singular series of beneficial accidents. Others say that we have no inherent value as individuals, but our value lies in disappearing into the universe's ultimate reality. Still, others say we have great value because the Creator/God loves us. Still, others say that our value is found in the community we are part of, or, as our existentialist friends tell us, the value of our lives is what we make it to be. If the postmodernist has a coherent view of the world, then all of these answers are equally valid. At face value, this answer from postmodernism is confusing at best. It is an answerless answer.

What is the nature of ultimate reality? Answer: It is what you say it is. And the more people you can find to agree with your understanding of ultimate reality, the more true it will become. What happens when we die? Answer: I am not sure. Where did I come from? Answer: you came from where you think you came from. These answers are not satisfactory. Postmodernism does a poor job of answering the questions that all of us want answers to.

Most concerning is postmodernism's answer to the question, What is the right thing to do? Postmodernism is not helpful when it comes to questions of morality. Moral truth, if it exists at all, comes from a higher authority. Morality comes from metanarrative, but metanarrative is the first target of postmodern thinking. Are any kinds of sexual activity moral? We can see where postmodernism is taking us here. The postmodern philosopher Michel Foucault "agonized profoundly over the question of whether rape should be regulated by penal justice."[37] Clearly, Foucault is an extreme outlier here. The truth remains, however. In a postmodern world, morality is all relative. If it is true for you but not for me, then if it is moral for you but not for me. This is moral relativism. What, then, happens to morality? The answer is that it disappears. Postmodernism is amoral. This is a problem.

Is Postmodernism Better?

Thus far, we have applied the "better" analysis only to materialism. Is postmodernism a better worldview than materialism? Can we reasonably predict that those who consistently apply this worldview to how they live

---

37 Ronald Beiner, "Foucault's Hyper-liberalism," *Critical Review,* Summer, 1995, 353-354.

their lives will be "better" than atheists? The answer is probably yes. Will the postmodern be "better" than the pantheist, the deist or the theist? We will see.

Can we reasonably anticipate that a consistent application of a postmodern perspective to how one lives his or her life will produce a humble, generous, courageous, diligent, self-controlled, honest, self-sacrificing person? Because all ideas about the ideal way of living and morality are subjective in postmodernism, the answer to this question will depend on the culture the individual is committed to. That being said, as a Christian theist, I believe that humans are made in the image of God and have a conscience that informs them of good and bad behavior. Nearly all humans have at least some sense of morality and ethics, reflected in our cultures. Virtually any system of values that the postmodern person accepts will come with a set of values.

I have heard it said many times that all religions are the same. A worldview analysis informs us that this is not even close to true. However, all religions have some sort of ethic and morality and the fact is that it is in this area, not in theology or worldview, that most religions are indeed at least somewhat similar. All religions agree that hatred, murder, greed, lying and other kinds of behavior are immoral. The postmodern may falsely believe that all truths are equal and that morality is "all relative." But at least most of them will hold to some system of morality. This is superior to the determinist who is committed to a worldview that says evil is not real, that our sense of the reality of moral systems is an ephemeral illusion, and that humans have no inherent value.

For example, as discussed above, one phenomenon of the postmodern world is the rapid rise in the "nones." These people, primarily young, claim to be spiritual but disavow all organized religion. Nothing could be more symptomatic of postmodernism than the rise of an eclectic, non-committed, but spiritual approach to life. When it comes to the question of better, surely it is preferrable for an individual to hold to at least some personal sense of spirituality, even with a vague sense of justice and morality than to hold to a purely materialist view of reality. I conclude that a postmodern world is "better" than an atheist world. But... a world in which moral ideas are "all relative" is not good. From a Christian point of view, it is not a moral world. It may even be a dangerous world.

Postmodernists prefer community to the radical individualism of the modernist. Postmodernists seek consensus and value tolerance. They tend to despise racism and most forms of bigotry. These are good qualities that make for better people than the alternative, which is modernism. They have taught us to listen to multiple perspectives—not to prefer Western to Eastern or Northern to Southern ways of thinking. Again, this is surely a good thing, and we can reasonably presume that it leads to a better person than alternatives such as extreme nationalism, racism, or cultural snobbery.

But is postmodernism the best worldview in the sense that it will produce the most self-controlled, least selfish, most honest, peace-loving, and compassionate person possible? We have a few more worldviews to analyze, but my preliminary answer is certainly not. Postmodernists value cultural conformity over those who take a strong stand for truth. In human history, the great heroes have stood up to oppose accepted truths. The most incredible humans have been revolutionaries. They are people who have spoken truth to power. They have done what postmodernists are averse to doing. They have told the majority in their native culture that certain accepted behaviors are wrong.

Names that come to mind include Nelson Mandela, Mother Theresa, Martin Luther King, and, let us not forget, the most conspicuous member of the revolutionary social club, Jesus of Nazareth. Postmodernists are skeptical of heroes—not of heroes who save other people from imminent danger, but of individuals who lay their lives on the line to proclaim that certain cultural norms are wrong. Cultural values are wrong if they violate basic human dignity, destroy families, are greedy, or use violence toward their ends. And the hero demands that we stop such behavior. Enough! They say. This is what biblical prophets always did. Our world desperately needs social and moral revolutionaries like Moses and Esther, Mandela, and Mother Theresa. Postmodernism will produce few, if any, of these. When it comes to an analysis of whether postmodernism is better, this fact is a severe problem. Postmodernism is better than materialism, but it certainly is not the superior view of the world.

SEVEN

Animism/Polytheism/Dualism

The stated intent of this book is to define and describe the major worldviews in the world today and to analyze whether they are a "good" view of the world. The subsequent major worldview we will be exploring is pantheism/Eastern religion. But before we do that, we will spend time in this chapter looking at some worldviews which have historically preceded the genesis of pantheistic religious systems but which are relatively uncommon today. These worldviews are receding in importance over time. In this chapter, we will look at animism, polytheism, and dualism. Anthropologists tell us that most ancient peoples were animists, but as cultures developed, they tended to move toward polytheism or dualism. So, we will start with animism.

Animism

What is animism? It is a self-defining term, as the root of the word is *anima*, a Latin word meaning breath or soul. The word animism was invented in the nineteenth century in Western Europe to describe an observed set of religious ideas or a worldview that Europeans discovered in their empire-building conquests. No one has ever called themselves an animist. When we discuss animism, we may want to be aware of Western chauvinistic attitudes toward non-Western ways of thinking. The term has carried a negative connotation from its conception. Let us use it advisedly. Nevertheless, we need a definition.

Animism is the idea that everything in the universe contains breath or soul.

Everything is animated. Everything, including trees, animals, mountains, rivers, and heavenly objects, have a soul or spirit. To the animist, there is almost no distinction between the physical and the spiritual world. In addition, to the animist, everything that happens has spiritual meaning. The animist world is magical. Rain has spiritual significance and cause, as do thunder and lightning. When we hear that ancient peoples worshipped mountains as holy places, this is evidence that those people were animists. To the animist, the "spirit" can be impersonal. It can be like a substance that imbues everything with significance. Or the spirits may be localized individual entities. A spiritual force or a soul might be located in a cave, on a mountaintop, or in some other "holy" place.

Obviously, animism takes a variety of forms. Typically, animistic religion involves obeying certain taboos to avoid offending spirits. Or it might include fetishes or charms, which are physical acts or objects which have spiritual effects. These fetishes might include sacrifices designed to appease the spirits and bring physical blessings to humans. In an animist world, there are many demons. The spirit world is controlled by specialists such as "witch doctors" or brujas.

Animism has yet to completely disappear in the Western world, despite the dominance of the modern mindset. It is not uncommon for people to look to the "primitive" for a sense of purpose and security. When I share my faith on campus, I come across some who call themselves pagans. They may associate themselves with ancient druidic religion. These "pagans" are animists.

I will not, at this time, subject animism to our worldview analysis. Science has informed us that unchanging natural laws govern physical reality. Nature is not magical. Weather and the motion of heavenly objects, eclipses, and comets are predictable. Animism cannot be taken seriously in the modern or even in the postmodern world. However, we should be aware as we discuss our worldview with people from sub-Saharan Africa, parts of Central America, and South Asia that many will have an animist perspective. Those converted to Islam, Hinduism, or Christianity from relatively "primitive" cultures will often carry their animism into their Islam, Hinduism, or Christianity. We may have to allow those converted from an animist religious perspective some space—some time to be changed from what appears to us to be a superstitious perspective.

Also, most of us with a Western background come from cultures that were, until recently, governed by a modernist, materialist perspective. We tend to deny the reality of angels and demons and to downplay spiritual forces and the possibility of the miraculous intervention of God into our reality. Those who come to Christianity from an animist perspective—whom we are inclined to think of as too superstitious—may be able to correct our overly skeptical, rationalist view of our own religion. As we Christians are told in the Bible, "Our struggle is not against flesh and blood, but against the rulers, against the authorities, against the powers of this dark world and against the spiritual forces of evil in the heavenly realms" (Ephesians 6:12).

Polytheism

We should be skeptical of religious anthropologists who tell us that there is a "natural" progression from animism to polytheism, to monotheism, deism, and, finally, materialism. We theists like to believe that we are theists, not because it is the next best thing after polytheism, but because it is an accurate view of the world. We believe in monotheism because it is true. Yet, there is a grain of truth in the idea that in ancient times less-developed, nomadic, agrarian, or hunter-gatherer groups tended more toward animism. In contrast, more developed cultures that inhabit cities and walled towns generally accept a polytheistic or dualistic worldview. Polytheism is more abstract than animism. It is less well-connected to nature and more connected to persons. Here is the definition.

Polytheism is the worldview that the universe is governed by a variety of supernatural persons that are called gods (with a small g). Such gods have human-like characteristics. They have personalities, self-awareness, and a will and interfere in human affairs.

We have described the Genesis creation account as a polemic against the Babylonian worldview. This worldview was polytheistic. To the Babylonian, humans lived in a world governed by deities such as Marduk, Tiamat, and Ea, as well as goddesses such as Ishtar. The principal worldview opponent throughout the Old Testament is the polytheistic religions of Israel's neighbors Egypt, Assyria, the Canaanites, the Philistines, the Ammonites, and the Hittites.

Those who accept a polytheistic worldview have several things in common. First, they believe that humans exist to serve the gods and not vice versa. Second, their world is essentially chaotic because it is influenced by a variety of capricious gods who have different personalities and compete for control of the world and the worship of humans. Third, their primary form of worship is sacrifice in temples to appease the various gods. Fourth, worship of deities/gods generally involves using physical idols as earthly channels or avatars which aid in accessing invisible gods.

This is the religion of the Aztecs, the Maya, and the Incas, as well as the ancient Egyptians, Mesopotamians, Romans, Greeks, and the Norse and Germanic peoples. It was also the religion of the old Indus Valley and, to a lesser extent, in ancient China. Polytheism is a major part of Hinduism as practiced in the Indian subcontinent today.

As with animism, we will not subject polytheism to a complete worldview analysis. There is a reason polytheism has lost out to pantheism and theism over time. A simple view of nature might make polytheism seem consistent with our observations. The weather certainly seems, at times to be chaotic and inherently unpredictable. Eclipses seem to come out of nowhere, and surely no "natural" law can explain them. The first big blow against the polytheistic worldview came from the Greek natural philosopher Thales of Miletus. Through careful observation of the sun and the moon and using some relatively sophisticated mathematics, he publicly predicted a total solar eclipse that happened on May 28, 585 BC. In doing so, Thales proved that natural philosophy and mathematics could be used to explain what all humans up to that time had assumed to be due to supernatural forces. This was the opening blow of a battle that eventually ended polytheism in Greece. Less than two hundred years after Thales' triumph, Greek intellectuals had already rejected their polytheism. We have already seen Aristophanes writing, "Shrines! Shrines! Surely you don't believe in the gods. What's your argument? Where's your proof?" Sixteen centuries after Thales, Christian monotheism produced science, and science has been fantastically successful in explaining the natural world. The universe is predictable. It is ordered—governed by natural laws. With its unavoidable prediction of a chaotic and unpredictable world, polytheism no longer works. It is not consistent with observable reality. Polytheism is on its last legs.

The word polytheism is not in either the Qur'an or the Bible. Yet, in both the Qur'an and the Old Testament, the most prevalent sin is idolatry. An idol is a physical object taken to represent a god or as a channel or avatar to access that god's power. As such, the prohibition of idolatry in these monotheistic religions is a condemnation of polytheism.

Dualism

Another worldview—one which can be thought of as a bridge between polytheism and monotheism—is dualism. There are at least two kinds of dualism. There is the philosophical or metaphysical dualism of Descartes, who distinguished two completely separate realities of mind and matter. This is not the dualism we are calling a worldview in this section. The other kind of dualism is religious dualism. Let us start with a definition.

Dualism is a view that two opposed supreme supernatural powers govern the universe.

Typical religious dualism involves an eternal battle between a spiritual force for good and one for evil.

In New Testament times, dualism was a significant alternative worldview in the Mediterranean world. Two of the most influential dualistic religions in the Near East originated in Persia. They were Zoroastrianism and Manichaeism. Zoroastrianism was the national religion of Persia during the Achaemenid dynasty, begun by Cyrus the Great, as well as during the Parthian and Sassanid dynasties. It dominated Persia, or present-day Iran, from the sixth century BC until the Muslim conquests in the early seventh century AD. Zoroastrianism was heavily persecuted in Persia under the Muslims, causing many to flee to the east. It exists today as a relatively minor religious movement in India, where these religious exiles are called Parsis. The number is somewhere less than 200,000. Zoroaster, also known as Zarathustra, the semi-mythical founder of Zoroastrianism, described a universe governed by the powers of good and evil, personified in the Zoroastrian God, Ahura Mazda, and the spirit of evil, Ahriman. This is classic dualism.

Two dualistic religious movements competed with Christianity in the first four centuries. These were Gnosticism and Manichaeism. Gnosticism proposed a dualism of matter which was corrupt and evil,and spirit, which is good. The Gnostic *Gospel of Judas* made the God of the Old Testament the Creator of a corrupt physical reality and the God of the New Testament a purely spiritual, good God. This good God created an emanation, personified in Jesus Christ. The most significant heretical teaching within second-century Christianity was dualistic Gnosticism. The Nag Hamadi Library, discovered in Egypt in 1945, contained a treasure trove of both dualistic non-Christian and "Christian" gnostic writings.

Manichaeism was founded by the Persian prophet Mani in the third century AD. It became a chief competitor to the growing Christian church both in the Roman empire and the East. It remained a powerful religious force from Rome to China until the eighth century, surviving as a very small and persecuted group in China up to modern times. The essence of this religion was a complex dualistic cosmology that described the world as an unending struggle between a spiritual world of light and a physical, evil world of darkness. As mentioned earlier, Augustine was the most important convert to the Manichee faith. He later left the religion to become, first, a Neoplatonist, then eventually, a Christian. Historians of Christianity see a remnant of Augustine's dualistic Manichaeism in his asceticism and his belief that all forms of pleasure are evil. This, in turn, influenced Western Christianity for many centuries.

Dualism has played a role in historic Christianity. The Bogomils were a neo-Gnostic Christian group that emerged in the tenth century in what we call Macedonia and Bulgaria today. Their view of reality described a world within the human body and a separate world outside the body. God created the human soul, but Satan created matter and the body. They rejected much of ecclesiastical Orthodox Christianity and had many practices for purifying the body.

Another dualistic sect of Christianity arose in Southern France in the twelfth and thirteenth centuries, known as the Cathars. Their anthropology was derived from the Manichaeans. They taught that there are two principles—one good and spiritual and one which is material and evil. The Roman Catholic Church used the Dominican friars to suppress the Cathari viciously, wiping out the population of entire cities, including some who were Orthodox in belief. The area of Provence, France was virtually depopulated.

The dualism in Chinese religion is more conceptual than theological. Traditional Chinese religion separates all qualities into yin and yang. Chinese dualism is more about the balance between opposing qualities than a battle between good and evil. Yin is the receptive principle, and yang is the active principle: winter versus summer, female versus male, and chaos versus order.

Is religious dualism a good worldview? Is it true, does it provide reasonable answers to the critical questions, and will it logically produce better people? Will the main idea of reality as a perpetual battle between more physical forces of evil and more spiritual forces of good hold up to what we learn from science? This seems unlikely. Is matter essentially corrupt and evil? How can an atom, a rock, a planet, or, for that matter, a human body be evil? Christianity views evil as the corruption of something which was created good. Materialism denies the reality of evil entirely. Dualism proposes that evil was created by God or by one of two competing Gods.

Is my body the product of random processes, acting over significant periods (materialism)? Is it a truly wondrous and beautiful thing, created to be enjoyed and to give glory to its Creator (Christian theism), or is it an inherently evil thing? Is pleasure inherently wrong? What is the psychological effect of believing that I, a good person, am trapped in an evil body? Is this a worldview that will produce better people than others? Will a dualistic worldview create a humble, generous, courageous, diligent, self-controlled, honest, self-sacrificing person? Maybe so. Undoubtedly better than morality-free materialism or radically relativist postmodernism. But an other-worldly worldview that denies the beauty inherent in creation will not tend to produce a person who has compassion for the sick, the weak, the outcast, or the disabled and the mentally ill. It is certainly not the best worldview one can imagine.

EIGHT

Pantheism-Monism/Panentheism

The next worldview we will consider is the dominant one in the East. It has had a growing influence in the West as well. Close to 1.8 billion people, or 20% of the world's population today, consider themselves part of a religion that is pantheist or monist in worldview.[38] This includes Hindus, Buddhists, Taoists, Jains, and a loosely-aligned religious movement in the West called New Age. If the entertainment culture in the United States and Europe has a religious perspective, it is more or less pantheistic. The worldview of *Star Wars, Pandora,* and *The Matrix* is pantheist.

First, let us provide definitions. But such definitions require we develop an Eastern vocabulary. The pantheism of Buddhism is not identical to that of Hinduism or Taoism. Hinduism is a highly diverse set of religions, which Westerners have described as a single religion only in recent times. Hinduism, as practiced today, evolved in ancient times from relatively primitive animism. By the second millennium BC, religions in the Indian subcontinent had grown to several related polytheistic beliefs, with literally thousands of gods, many of which are still worshipped today. In the first millennium BC, it evolved into a syncretistic religion which is essentially pantheistic in its worldview but still included the worship of many gods. Pantheism is found in the early Hindu scriptures. This is true to some extent in the Vedas (1500-1000 BC), but especially in the Upanishads (800-600 BC), as well as in the epics such as the Ramayana, Mahabharata, and Bhagavad Gita. With its many regional and national gods, a vast array of practices, and extensive Scripture, Hinduism is a very complicated religion. But this is a book of worldviews, not world religions. Our present task is the simpler one of describing and analyzing the underlying pantheism in Hinduism.

---

38   Religious Composition by Country, 2010-2050". "Religious Composition by Country, 2010-2050," Pew Research Center. 2 April 2015.

Unlike Hinduism, Buddhism has a definite place, time, and person to which we can trace its origin. The site is in north-central India, and the person is Siddhartha Gautama, who lived from about 566 to about 486 BC. He started an ascetic movement in North India which he conceived as a middle path between the extreme worldliness of Hinduism and the extreme asceticism of the Jains. This ought to make it easier to describe the worldview of Buddhism. But nothing about the Buddha was put to pen until three hundred years after his death.

Additionally, Buddhism divided very early into Theravada (Lesser vehicle) and Hinayana (Greater vehicle) sects, with significantly different worldviews. Zen Buddhism in Japan and Tantric Buddhism in Tibet are about as different as night and day. Yet, both are pantheist in worldview. Add to this ambiguity, Siddhartha Gautama, the founder of Buddhism, adamantly refused to commit to a view of ultimate reality publicly, making it hard to pin down his worldview. Some have described him as agnostic or even atheist. Such is not the case, and we can be assured that the worldview of the Buddha was pantheist.

The pantheism of the Jain religion is somewhat different as well. This extremely ascetic religion was founded by Mahavira (about 599-527 BC). Its practice is opposed to Hinduism, but its cosmology and worldview have much in common with Hinduism and Buddhism. It is pantheist. Many have suggested that Siddhartha Gautama met Mahavira. Chinese Taoism has been called pantheistic, but it is better to use the term panentheism (defined below).

We have to start somewhere. We will use Hindu vocabulary to provide a basic definition of pantheism. The Sanskrit word for the human soul is atman. The Sanskrit word for God or the universal soul/reality is Brahman. We will use a statement from the Hindu Scripture known as the Upanishads to define monism or pantheism. In the Upanishads, we read:

"Atman is Brahman."

This, in a pithy saying, is a Hindu way of describing pantheism. We will see that Buddhists have different vocabulary for talking pantheistically. The same goes for Jains. They are different, but they are more similar than different in worldview. What is a human being? The answer is that atman is Brahman. To use Western language, in pantheism, a human being is God. I am God. You are God. We are God, and God is us. A goal of Hinduism is to discover our inner god-self. But we must still be cautious about vocabulary. The Hindu concept of God is very different from theism. To the Hindu, God or Brahman is the one, infinite, impersonal, ultimate reality. This is why Hinduism is described as a pantheistic or monist religion—because in Hinduism, "God" is not a person. To overly simplify, in the pantheistic religions, Jain, Buddhism, and Hinduism, God is the universe, and the universe is God. God is all (and thus the word pantheism), and everything is God (and hence the word monism). The entire universe is one thing.

Pantheism: God is the one, infinite, impersonal, all-encompassing, ultimate reality.

Buddhist pantheism is similar but not the same as that in Hinduism. The monist reality in Buddhism is not a thing called Brahman. It is a void or nothingness. The Hindu goal is to be dissolved into Brahman—for atman to become Brahman. The Buddhist goal is to be dissolved into the universal void. The goal for humans is to become non-beings.[39] In Hinduism, a person is an illusory thing, but in Buddhism, a person is a not-soul. As we do a worldview analysis of pantheism, this distinction will have a relatively small significance in our true, right, better analysis, but we should be aware of the difference.

The distinction between pantheism/monism and panentheism will seem small to Western eyes. Ancient Greek Stoicism and traditional Chinese Taoism have been described as having a panentheist worldview. Pantheism equates the universe with God. Brahman is all, and all is Brahman. Panentheism is a worldview that sees all being in God. In other words, all the world is in God, but God is larger than the world. The universe is one (and thus monism), but God transcends the universe and has an existence above or beyond the universe. In this chapter, for the sake of simplicity and at the risk of offending some, I will treat pantheism and panentheism as one (pun intended).

We are about to analyze pantheism, but I will share a personal story first. I was raised with a theistic worldview. By college, I had left Christianity and labeled myself an atheist. Due to my discovery of apparent design in nature as a science student, but also through some personal mystical experiences, I left my worldliness behind to seek God. However, the first stop on my religious journey led me to pantheism. I was attracted to Hinduism, especially the variety found in the West. I read the

---

39   Robert Linssen, *Zen: The Art of Life* (New York: Pyramid, 1962), p. 142-143.

writings of Paramahansa Yogananda and the American Ram Das eagerly. I was fascinated with the book *Siddhartha* by Herman Hesse. This novel, trendy in the 1970s, is a Western retelling of the life of Siddhartha Buddha. I became a vegetarian and practiced a form of meditation. I found the idea that I am a personal God-containing vessel attractive. Only after a couple of years did I start reading the Bible and reject pantheism (though I would not have described it that way at the time). I was not alone. In the 1970s in Boulder, Colorado, there were many Buddhist groups, as well as Hare Krishnas and practitioners of Transcendental Meditation.

Is It True?

We will now do the principal task of this book, which is to ask if Pantheism is a "good" worldview. First, let us ask the simple question: Is pantheism true? Do the basic facts about the universe align with the assumption that all is God? The answer, plain and simple, is that pantheism is not true for more than one reason.

First, there is the cosmology of pantheism. This worldview requires that humans, nature, and prime reality all be one. The God of pantheism is impersonal and is contained in the universe itself. If this is the case, then we can be sure that God did not create the universe. Pantheism is simply incompatible with a created universe. The universe cannot create itself. If we look not at the theology but at the cosmologies of all Eastern pantheistic religions, they are very similar. The cosmology of Hinduism involves repeating cycles of creation, destruction, and recreation. The "trinity" of Hinduism is Brahma (not Brahman), the creator; Vishnu, the sustainer; and Shiva, the destroyer. Every turn of the cosmic wheel involves the physical universe being recreated out of pre-existent stuff. Brahma creates, Vishnu sustains, and Shiva destroys.

With the vast array of Hindu Scripture, one will discover more than one version of Hindu cosmology. One describes a single cycle of the wheel of time as lasting 100 "Brahma years," which is many trillions of years, after which the physical universe is destroyed by Shiva and recreated by Brahma. In addition, all Hindu cosmologies have reality being composed of different "levels" of reality, with the lower levels being more physical and therefore more evil, and the higher levels being less physical—more spiritual, and thus less evil (see the illustrations). In Hinduism, material things are an illusion (maya), and the more material things are evil. As in Greek philosophies, Hinduism sees physical creation as corrupted and evil.

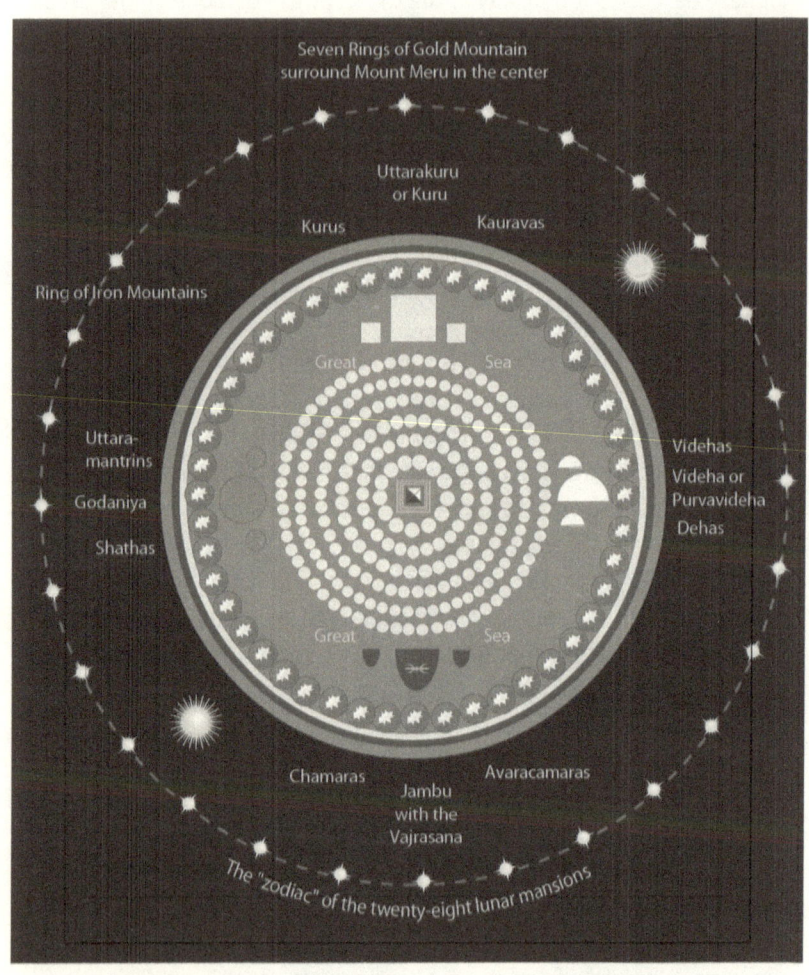

Seven Rings of Gold Mountain
surround Mount Meru in the center

Uttarakuru
or Kuru

Kurus   Kauravas

Ring of Iron Mountains

Great   Sea

Uttara-
mantrins

Godaniya

Shathas

Great   Sea

Videhas

Videha or
Purvavideha

Dehas

Chamaras   Avaracamaras

Jambu
with the
Vajrasana

The "zodiac" of the twenty-eight lunar mansions

A diagram of Hindu cosmology, with many levels of increasingly less physical reality.

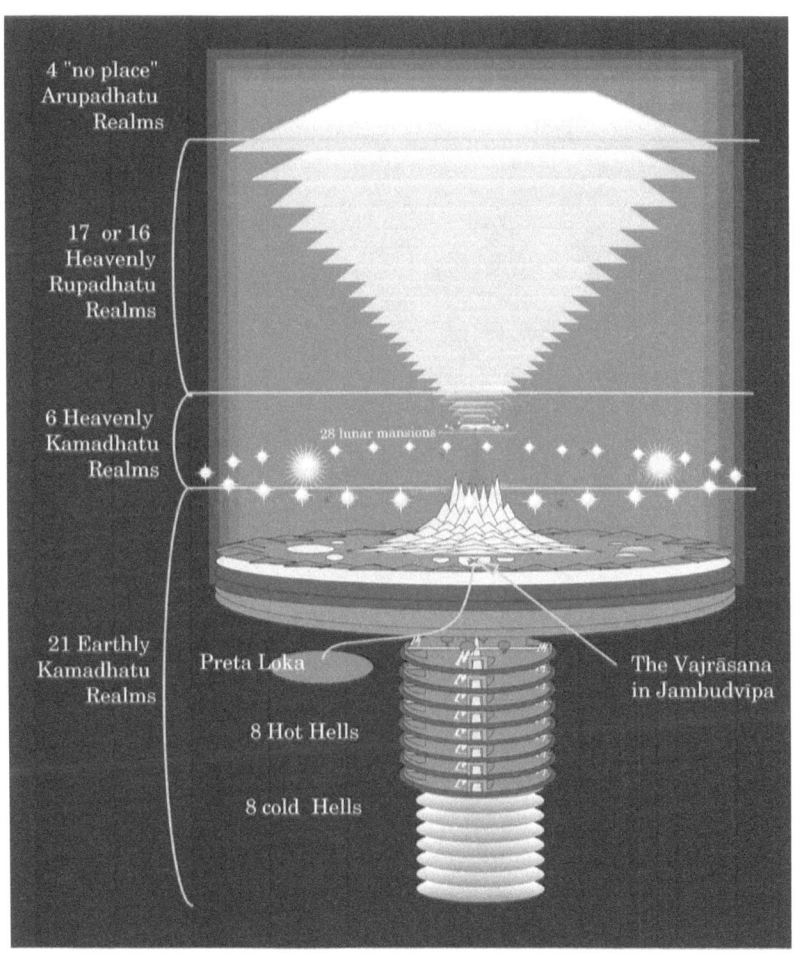

This is a picture of a Buddhist cosmology.

Angkor Wat in Cambodia: a phyysical representation of Hindu cosmology

Borobudur Temple in Java, Indonesia: A physical representation of
Buddhist cosmology with its many layers of reality.

There is a reason all pantheist cosmologies have both an unending cyclic "wheel" of time and multiple levels of reality. In pantheism, it is a logical imperative that the universe be eternal. It cannot have been created. A thing cannot create itself; in pantheism, the universe and God are one. In pantheism, we progress from lower to higher levels of existence or regress from higher to lower levels of existence.

There is a big problem with this cosmology. Science is clear on this. The second law of thermodynamics tells us that, over time, the universe gets colder as entropy increases. The universe we live in will wear out over time. If the universe were infinitely old, it would be infinitely cold. In addition, as mentioned earlier, the evidence is clear. The big bang model works. The universe was created. There was a time when it was not. We cannot have it both ways. Pantheism is disproved. We can discuss the nature of the Creator. Or we might even consider the atheist idea of a self-initiated universe. Still, pantheism, by definition, tells us that everything is God, and therefore, God did not create the universe. But the evidence suggests differently, which means that pantheism is not true.

There are other aspects common to religions that have a pantheistic worldview. Are these aspects of pantheistic worldviews true? All propose that physical things are corrupted and evil. Is this true? Is it true that matter and those humans more closely tied to matter are, in some sense, bad? All pantheistic religions propose a cosmology that consists of multiple levels of reality, with some lower levels being more evil and "higher" levels being less corporeal. This begs the question: Is there any evidence whatsoever for these different levels of reality? The answer is a clear no. We may be attracted to the pantheistic proposal that we are God at our center, but this idea has implications which are simply untrue. They are not consistent with observable reality.

Whether we are talking about Jain, Buddhism, Hinduism, or Western New Age religion, one common tie is a belief in the soul's reincarnation. As does the universe, Individuals go through multiple cycles of birth, death, and reincarnation. This religious claim raises real problems. Anthropologists estimate that roughly one-third to one-fourth of all humans who have ever lived are alive right now. If this is true, how can each living human have gone through dozens or hundreds of previous incarnations? If we talk to our New Age friends, they are convinced that they had earlier lives as kings, queens, significant literary figures, or other people of importance. Statistics tell us that this is a logical impossibility. Reincarnation is a nice idea, but the reincarnation of the pantheist religions today is untrue.

Is It Right?

All worldviews provide answers to the most basic questions that humans need to be answered. Are those answers consistent with reality, do they make sense, and are they satisfactory? Let it be said first that pantheistic Eastern religions give better answers to these questions than either materialism or postmodernism. Pantheism has a morality similar to Christian theism. Pantheism also proposes a purpose and meaning to life.

Why am I here?
What is my purpose?
How did I get here?
What is my value?
What is a human being?
What is the right thing to do?
Is or will there be ultimate justice?
What is the nature of ultimate reality?
What happens to me when I die?

What is the purpose of life? What is the path toward which humans, ideally, are moving? In Hinduism, the goal is to reach the state of nirvana. The word has a very positive connotation in English, but what is the state of nirvana? It is a state of non-existence. It is a state of having been reabsorbed into the universal cosmic entity. It is a state in which atman has become brahman. The goal is to cease to exist as an individual. In Hinduism, the individual is not of great inherent value. The goal is for the individual to no longer exist as an individual.

In Buddhism, the purpose and goal of life are similar but not the same. Siddhartha said that the ultimate goal that humans ought to strive for is not-being. It is to be dissolved back into the void. I am sorry, but to me, that is not a good goal for life. Call me selfish if you like, but I am not drawn to the idea that my ultimate goal is to no longer exist—to disappear. If it is true, I suppose I will have to accept the truth grudgingly, but I am not attracted to this idea.

What is my value? Again, in pantheistic religions, the individual has minimal value, as the goal of these religions is to no longer be an individual. There is a kind of afterlife in pantheistic religions, but this afterlife involves a cycle of birth, death, and reincarnation, with the hope of escaping this cycle. This idea of reincarnation raises problems.

What is the right thing to do? All pantheistic religions have a system of moral truth, and these moral truths are not vastly different from theistic religions such as Islam, Judaism, or Christianity. This is good. The ideas of morality in Buddhist countries such as Thailand, Myanmar, and India are familiar to those in Christianity. They agree that violence is evil and that dishonesty is reprehensible. In Hinduism, evil acts accrete bad karma. To proceed to higher, less physical levels or being, one must accumulate good karma and avoid acts such as selfishness that bring bad karma. It is a sort of what Christians might call "works salvation." There is also a sense of justice in this worldview, as those who do evil suffer the consequences by being reincarnated in a lower state—perhaps even as an animal. This motivates living as good people. It is a positive for pantheism.

Pantheism struggles a bit with the question, "Why am I here?" Why do I exist at all? In an impersonal reality, why do persons exist? And how is it that individual persons, who appear to have free will arise out of an impersonal One who, being impersonal, has no will? So far, I have not heard a good answer to this question.

Is It Better?

If pantheism does better than naturalism and postmodernism on whether it is right, it also does better on our third measure of a good worldview. A world with no morality, or one with a very confusing morality, does not naturally produce humble, generous, courageous, diligent, self-controlled, honest, and self-sacrificing people. Those who are consistent and dedicated followers of Buddhism, Jain, and Hinduism are more likely to be humble than those who do not. Buddhism, with its eight-fold path, definitely teaches self-control, and honesty is valued for ethical and moral reasons.

But pantheism has some significant drawbacks which ought to be exposed. In Hinduism, as in Buddhism, physical reality is not truly real. The physical is an illusion. It is *maya*, which means illusion. In both religions, only the ultimate One is good. Therefore, in pantheist religions, evil, suffering, and even death are illusions—they are *maya*. This is problematic. If individuals are, in some sense, not real, and if suffering is an illusion, what ought people to do about a thing such as suffering which is not real? The imperative to help those suffering is, at best, weak in pantheistic cultures. Pantheists tell us that evil is not real. Really? It sure seems real to me. Rape and incest are just plain evil. If evil is not real, does this create a strong motivation for us to help prevent other people from doing evil? Might this partially explain some of the prevalent evils in the Indian subcontinent?

Consider the nation of India. Christians make up somewhere between one and two percent of the inhabitants of the Indian subcontinent. Yet, if we travel to India, we will soon discover that much of the benevolent work there is done by Christians. Most of the hospitals, orphanages, and other non-governmental organizations to take care of the most basic needs, such as poverty, are run by theists, not by pantheists. This is not an accident. We can agree that many very nice Hindus care a lot about human suffering. Mahatma Gandhi is an excellent example, but their worldview does not strongly support this.

I have already stated that the eight-fold path of Buddhism includes some excellent goals. However, let us consider what the ultimate good of Buddhism is. The ultimate goal for human beings is to escape feelings and emotions. The goal is not compassion. The goal is dispassion and non-involvement in human affairs. This may explain why in Buddhist countries such as Sri Lanka, Thailand, and Viet Nam, as in India, Christian groups do benevolent works that far outweigh their proportion of the population. What the world needs now is love, sweet love, not dispassion, withdrawal, and an escape into the void.

Ultimately, pantheistic religions focus more on the self than the other. It is about a self-journey toward personal enlightenment. The journey is not one of compassion for our fellow humans. There is an element of selfishness there. In pantheism, it is not clear that the individual has a profound, inherent dignity. The ideal of individual dignity and human rights would never have originated in pantheist-dominated societies. This causes me to question whether pantheism, logically, will produce better human beings than, for example, theism.

New Age Religion

We have yet to consider Western forms of pantheism. Indian pantheism includes many gods and goddesses such as *Ganesha,* the elephant god of wisdom; *Lakshmi,* the goddess of wealth; or the chief female deity, *Devi,* the goddess of *shakti* or power. Hinduism, as practiced in India, includes music, incense, and sacrifices to these gods. It is a very physical, worldly worship. The list of gods in Hinduism is long and varied. Hinduism has also produced many avatars—human demigods who are physical manifestations of higher spiritual realities. These include Krishna and Rama—avatars of Vishnu. The unknowable, ineffable, impersonal One produces more personal emanations as a bridge between humans and the unknowable universal Brahman. The epics in Hinduism are myths about these avatars.

Buddhism is not as worldly as Hinduism, thanks to the influence of Siddhartha Gautama. It does not include gods, but Mahayana Buddhism does have its many bodhisattvas. These spiritually advanced god-like persons help humans on the path to enlightenment.

When pantheism came to the West in the nineteenth century, such gods were left behind in India. The pantheism adopted in the West is more esoteric and spiritual than what is practiced in India. It is not polytheistic. Arguably, this is a good thing! Pantheism in the West has sprung many philosophical/religious movements such as Theosophy, Eckankar, The Self-Realization Fellowship, the I AM religions, Hare Krishna, Transcendental Meditation, Hatha Yoga, and more.

By the late 1980s, a loosely-knit and eclectic home-grown pantheistic movement known as the New Age Movement coalesced and grew in prominence in the West in general, especially in the United States. Actress Shirley MacLaine became an influential spokesperson with her book *Out On a Limb* (1986). Also noteworthy for his public support for New Ageism is Deepak Chopra, MD. He has become an accepted spokesperson for New Age thinking. It is hard to nail down New Ageism, but let us try. Is New Age channeling? Is it seances? Is it palm-reading? Does it include meditation and reincarnation? Does it dabble in the occult, pyramid power, and crystals? What about using psychedelic drugs to open our minds to new realities? Does it have gurus? What about paganism and a dose of the mother goddess? Yes, Western New Age belief is all of these things, and it is more. It is Gnosticism, Spiritualism, Mysticism, Paganism, Buddhism, and Hinduism; all wrapped up in an attractive-looking package. It is incredibly eclectic. It is buffet-style religion.

Having said this, the heart of New Age thinking and practice is monistic pantheism. It is the idea that you and I are God. The goal is to discover our inner deity. I will let the New Age cultural guru Deepak Chopra speak for the movement:

> "Holding on to anything is like holding on to your breath. You will suffo-
> cate. The only way to get anything in the physical universe is by letting go of it.
> Let go and it will be yours forever."

> "There is no holy life. There is no war between good and evil. There is no
> sin and no redemption. None of these things matter to the real you. But they
> all matter hugely to the false you, the one who believes in the separate self.
> You have tried to take your separate self, with all its loneliness and anxiety and
> pride, to the door of enlightenment. But it will never go through because it is
> a ghost."

> "Once we begin to see that we are all God, then I think the whole purpose
> of life is to re-own the God-likeness within us."

This is pantheism, plain and simple. Pantheism has also made significant inroads in the West through yoga. Most Westerners think of yoga merely as a kind of exercise that promotes body awareness and mindfulness. If we look closely at both the practices of yoga and the underlying religious presuppositions of yoga, we will discover that the essence of the exercise program is a religious practice whose origins are found in pantheistic Hinduism. It promotes learning about the god that is hidden within. Yoga fits within the pantheistic worldview.

New Age religion falls in the pantheistic worldview, but it has its differences with religions that originated in Asia. First, being Western, it accepts that the physical world is real. In Eastern pantheism, physical reality is an illusion, and attachment to material things is, in essence, evil. The New Age worldview does not include this idea. This leads to inconsistency. But then, no one ever said that New Age ideas are coherent. If we accept what Deepak Chopra said, which is that we are all this pantheistic God, then the only reality is this spiritual, universal essence, which ought to imply that physical things are, at best, an illusion. New Age thinkers miss this inconsistency. They accept the reality of nature and the "truth" of natural laws.

Another enormous gulf between Western pantheism and that in the East is that being Western and largely an American product, it is very individualistic. Its goal is that each of us experiences our I AM self, our god-within. We need to discover that we are gods. Krishna is God, Jesus is God, the ascended masters are God, and you are God. Once again, this produces a self-contradictory worldview, as the One is an impersonal, ineffable essence, not a person, but New Ageism is highly focused on the individual.

A last thing to say before a very brief worldview analysis is this. New Age is a very attractive idea. It offers much but asks little. We learn that we are God. We know that all of life is about ourselves. There is no sin, and nothing to feel guilty about. We understand that we have infinite power and infinite possibility. It has not a hint of asceticism or self-denial. At its heart, Western pantheism, in its various New Age manifestations, is selfish religion based on a self-centered worldview.

Is this difficult-to-define, eclectic amalgamation of paganism, occultism, and pantheism we call New Age a good worldview? Let us assume, for argument, that we can establish its worldview. Let's ask our familiar questions. Is it true? Am I God? If our answer is yes, then this is pantheism (or possibly panentheism), and we have already shown above that pantheism inescapably requires a cosmology that cannot be true. It requires an eternal universe. Am I God? No, you are not! You did not, and you cannot create yourself. New Age pantheism is not true.

Is the New Age worldview right? Does it provide reasonable, consistent answers to the questions people care about? This is hard to answer because of the inherent inconsistencies in a worldview that believes in an impersonal, ineffable world-consciousness yet values and exalts the individual. Western pantheism, as practiced by those who fall under the New Age umbrella, needs to be clarified, and it provides, at best, confusing answers to the most basic questions. On the positive side, practitioners of Western pantheism generally abhor racism, nationalism, and greedy capitalism. They are usually tolerant (perhaps too tolerant?) and support efforts by humans to treat our environment wisely.

In the previous section, I gave positive credit to Eastern pantheism because these Eastern religions generally support the idea of moral ideals. In the New Age of the 21st century, this commitment to truth is weakened significantly. Let me repeat the earlier quote from Deepak Chopra, which does reflect quite accurately the general view of New Age authors:

> "There is no holy life. There is no war between good and evil. There is no sin and no redemption. None of these things matter to the real you. But they all matter hugely to the false you, the one who believes in the separate self.

> You have tried to take your separate self, with all its loneliness and anxiety and pride, to the door of enlightenment. But it will never go through because it is a ghost."

Here we see that the idea of evil is significantly downplayed in this movement. And there is no such thing as "sin." The only actual sin in New Age thinking is denying you are God. Sin is not selfishness or greed or dishonesty to your fellow human. It is denying your God-self.

Does this worldview make us better persons? Can we rationally predict that accepting this eclectic worldview will produce people who are more humble, generous, courageous, diligent, self-controlled, honest, and self-sacrificing? Of course, this depends on the worldview one is comparing it to. However, I can find nothing in the writings of New Age authors which makes me confident that this worldview produces self-sacrificing, humble people. If anything, it has a sense of arrogance in many. Here is a quote from New Age guru Shirley MacLaine:

> "If I created my own reality, then—on some level and dimension I didn't understand—I had created everything I saw, heard, touched, smelled, tasted; everything I loved, hated, revered, abhorred; everything I responded to or that responded to me. Then, I created everything I knew. I was therefore responsible for all there was in my reality... Was this what was meant by the statement I AM THAT I AM?"[40]

Never mind the possibly offensive coopting of Exodus 3:14; this statement has apparent hubris. Personal experience, combined with the writings of this new pantheism, informs me that the answer is no. Overall, this worldview does not produce others-centered, compassionate, unselfish, humble individuals. But time will tell because Western pantheism is an uncentered, evolving phenomenon.

---

40 Shirley MacLaine, *It's All in the Playing* (New York: Bantam, 1987), p. 192.

NINE

Deism

The worldview we call deism has already been discussed as the historical and logical step between biblical theism and materialism or even nihilism. It has been called "the isthmus between two great continents—theism and naturalism."[41] Historically, deism is the product of the late seventeenth and early eighteenth-century Enlightenment, especially in England and France. This was the age of Reason when the intellectual world shifted from focusing on special revelation as a source of truth to human reason. Deism is a "natural religion" which rejects the idea of revealed religion and special revelation. Deists claim that Reason (with a capital R) has the right and the duty to hold Special Revelation to account.[42] Roger E. Olson sums up the deistic perspective: "Nothing should be accepted as true by an intelligent being... unless it is grounded in the nature of things and is in harmony with right reason."[43]

We have already seen Descartes and Newton's role in creating deism. Let us look a bit deeper. Lord Herbert of Cherbury was known as the "Father of Deism." In the early seventeenth century, he published a list of five tenets that defined this system of religious thought.[44]

1. God exists.
2. We are required to give reverence to God.
3. Worship consists of pursuing practical morality.
4. We should repent of our sins.
5. We will receive divine recompense in the world according to how we live.

41 James W. Sire, *The Universe Next Door* (Downer's Grove, Il: InterVarsity, 2020), p. 55.

42 John Oakes, *The Christian Story: Finding the Church in Church History,* Vol. IV (Spring, TX: IPI, 2023)

43 Roger E. Olson, *The Story of Christian Theology* (Downers Grove, Illinois: Intervarsity Press, 1999). p. 520.

44 Lord Herbert, *De Veritate,* in Peter Gay, *Deism: An Anthology* (Anvil Books,1968), p. 32-38.

Theists will have no trouble with these tenets, but Cherbury stopped there. Anything beyond this must be reasonable. If it is not "reasonable," it is not true or Christian. Perhaps the most influential early work published to promote deistic thinking was that of the infamous skeptic John Toland, *Christianity not Mysterious,* in 1696. In this book, Toland proposed that "whoever reveals anything, that is, whoever tells us something we did not know before, his words must be intelligible, and the matter possible. This rule holds good; let God or Man be the revealer."[45]

Not all deists were skeptics. Not at all. John Locke considered himself a devoted Christian. He defended the reasonableness of Scripture, but he was a deist. Concerning the place of reason in Christianity, he said, "Whatever God has revealed is true and must be the object of our faith; but what actually counts as having been revealed by God, *that* must be judged by reason."[46] Historically, deism reached its peak influence in the eighteenth century. Important deists include Voltaire, Benjamin Franklin, and Thomas Jefferson.

By the early nineteenth century, as believers began to realize that deism was a slippery slope to skepticism and a complete rejection of moral truth, it lost steam. Europeans tended to either turn from doubt altogether, to reject deism and return to biblical theism, or embrace skepticism and become atheists. Like a sandbar between islands after a hurricane, the "isthmus" between Christian theism and materialism was eroded significantly. However, the deist worldview retains a small but significant number of believers. This is especially true among scientists, who are naturally drawn to natural religion. Famous modern deists include Charles Darwin and Albert Einstein. Concerning abiogenesis, Darwin said, "It is mere rubbish thinking, at present, of the origin of life; one might as well think of the origin of matter."[47] And Einstein said, "science without religion is lame; religion without science is blind." Einstein's God does not work miracles and does not intervene in the natural order, but the natural order cannot exist without a Creator. Another representative of deism is

---

45   John Toland, *Christianity Not Mysterious,* in Peter Gay, *Deism: An Anthology* (Anvil Books,1968), p. 61.

46   James M. Byrne, *Religion and the Enlightenment: From Descartes to Kant* (Louisville: Westminster John Knox Press, 1996), p. 107.

47   March, 1863, Darwin writing to his friend Joseph Hooker, about this inclusion of the three significant words "by the Creator" in Origin of Species.

Anthony Flew. Flew was perhaps the most notorious philosophical atheist in the last half of the 20th century. Shockingly, in 2004 Flew publicly switched his view, announcing his acceptance of what we call deism. Due to the apparent design in nature, he said that he "simply had to go where the evidence led.[48] I mentioned earlier my good friend Dick Albert, whom I labeled an atheist. After teaching our class Intro to Scientific Thought several times, he walked into my office one day in about 2012, "John! There is a Designer! God is real! Dick passed away a few years ago as a deist.

Enough of history, interesting as it may be. We need a simple statement of the deist worldview.

Deism: The belief in a single Creator who caused the universe but who does not intervene in his creation.

This is a God who does not work miracles, which would break his natural laws. This is a God who does not answer prayer. This is a relatively impersonal God. This is a God who only reveals himself through General Revelation and natural human reason—not through Special Revelation. Deists deny the trinity as not a reasonable proposal. Deists are divided on the reality of life after death. However, they tend to be united that hell is not reasonable (Lord Herbert of Cherbury above being an exception). Therefore, deists either deny life after death, or they are Universalists like Joseph Priestley. Priestley was a scientist, a friend of Benjamin Franklin, and founder of what became the Unitarian Universalist Church. The Unitarian Universalist Church is deist in worldview.

It is time to ask whether Deism is a "good" worldview. Let me reveal the answer before I start. Most Deists is the best worldview we have looked at so far, other than Christian theism.

Is It True?

In this book, we consider a worldview to be true if it is consistent with what appear to be facts about reality in the universe. We are applying the correspondence theory of truth. As for this measure of a "good" worldview, deism fares far better than any of the previous worldviews we have examined. The cosmology of deism agrees with most or perhaps even all of what has been observed empirically about the universe. Unlike

48   Anthony Flew with Abraham Varghese, *There is a God: How the World's Most Notorious Atheist Changed His Mind* (San Francisco: HarperOne, 2007)

materialism, animism, polytheism, dualism, and pantheism, it is clear that the deistic presupposition implies a universe created out of nothing. Scientific evidence agrees with this prediction. In this sense, deism is a good worldview.

One area where deists may get into trouble is in explaining the existence of life. A strongly-held deistic position is that God created the universe like a machine. He wound it up and let it go. If so, life, which came into existence after the universe, ought to result from entirely natural processes. The coldest version of deism implies that God did not directly create life but that it was created naturally by the universe which God created. This would imply abiogenesis. But, as I showed earlier, abiogenesis is almost certainly untrue.

But then again, most deists do not go to the logical extreme of their worldview. Many deists allow their God a minimal amount of intervention in his creation. For example, the group known as *Biologos* is an influential organization of believers trying to bridge the gap between mainstream Christianity and science. This organization proposes that God intervenes in nature rarely, if at all. To *Biologos*, evolution is an entirely natural process. They believe in a deistic evolution, but the creation of life itself and the design of *homo divinus*—of mankind in the image of God—is a unique, supernatural intervention.

This begs the question of whether God does intervene in nature at various times for his own purposes. Is the process of change of species over time an entirely random process as deists propose? Or does God intervene from time to time to direct evolution toward his pre-determined end? This question will not be resolved in this book. Let me say this. I am a theistic, not a deistic evolutionist. I believe God does at times intervene in his physical creation to perform supernatural acts we call miracles. I believe that, consistent with his interaction with his creation in other areas, God has intervened and directed evolution toward the creation of highly intelligent beings. The evidence is consistent with this idea. However, I am not prepared to label the deistic notion of evolution as "not true." Let us say that the jury is out on this question.

And what about the question of miracles such as those clearly described in the Bible? Miracles—defined as events in the physical world that violate natural law—do they indeed happen? Again, we will not resolve the question in this book. Let us say this. If you are personally convinced that God does miracles—that he intervenes directly in the lives of human beings—then you will call deism untrue. Or put it another way. If the Bible is inspired by God and is a reliable source of truth about human history, then deism is untrue.

Whereas pantheism leads to the idea that physical things are ephemeral and not truly "real" and are associated with evil, deism implies that the created world is real and is inherently good. Again, this is consistent with reality. Atoms are real, as are stars, light, and all the other stuff of physical reality. On this point, deism also appears to be true and, therefore, a good worldview.

Is It Right?

Does deism provide satisfactory answers to the questions that all human beings earnestly desire to be answered?

> Why am I here?
> What is my purpose?
> How did I get here?
> What is my value?
> What is a human being?
> What is the right thing to do?
> Is or will there be ultimate justice?
> What is the nature of ultimate reality?
> What happens to me when I die?

As with the question of whether it is true, deism rises to the top on this question when compared to the previous worldviews. What is our value? Deists, like theists, believe that humans have inherent worth and dignity from their Creator. They think that creation is about a God who wanted to create us as the highest revelation of his being. After all, the deist Thomas Jefferson wrote the famous words, "We hold these truths to be self-evident: All men were created equal."

Having said this, deism does pose some problems with the question of human significance. If the universe is closed because its Creator does not intervene, then there is a sense in which deism implies determinism. What does this do to human significance? As James Sire has said, "People become cogs in the clockwork mechanism of the universe. Human significance and mechanical determinism are impossible bedfellows."[49] This is something to ponder.

On the question of morality, deism struggles as well, at least in comparison to theism. What is the right thing to do? The deist applies the precepts of human reason to evaluate whether something in the Bible is true. To the deist, what is moral is what is consistent with human reason, not necessarily what is in the Bible. The problem with this is that humans always have differing views on what is reasonable. One person's "reasonable" moral truth is not the same as another's. Almost by definition, absolute moral truth derives from a supernatural being who determines this truth and, hopefully, communicates that truth to human beings. But, because of their worldview, deists have rejected authoritative Scripture. This is what Europeans discovered in the second half of the nineteenth century. Deism is a fragile vessel to support morality.

Deists agree that human consciousness is real. They agree that we are persons. This is good. However, deism either downplays or denies the providence of God. In a deistic world, God does not intervene in history or individuals' lives. Deism needs help explaining or even agreeing with the concept of free will. In a world where God does not act as a sovereign person, it is challenging to define free will. Deists can agree with theists that evil is the corruption of something good that God created. To this extent, Deists have a proper understanding of evil. Deism can rightly describe the problem of evil, but deism does a relatively poor job or explaining history. Redemption involves God intervening in human history, which deists reject a priori. Deism can "explain" the death of Christ, but it denies his resurrection. From a Christian perspective, accepting the death of Christ for redemption, but denying his resurrection is confusing if not downright contradictory.

One more question for deism as a worldview. If, as deists propose, an all-powerful, all-knowing, all-good God exists, why would he create conscious humans with the power to speak and never speak to them? As James Anderson put it, "not even a quick 'hello.'"[50]

Is It Good?

What does common sense tell us? Will a life consistent with a deistic

---

49   James W. Sire, *The Universe Next Door* (Downer's Grove, Il: InterVarsity, 2020), p. 53.

50   James N. Anderson, *What's Your Worldview?* (Wheaton, Il: Crossway, 2014), p. 61.

view of the world naturally produce a humble, generous, courageous, diligent, self-controlled, honest, and self-sacrificing person?

In a deistic world, moral questions are a matter of human reason. If God does not reveal himself except through General Revelation, what is the basis for establishing absolute moral truth? If there is no basis for deciding right and wrong other than human reasoning, does this create a solid basis for moral and ethical living? We should be skeptical of this prospect. Is a deistic world one in which we will want to live?

In the final analysis, much or all of the morality that deists defend derives from the theism from which it sprung. Like present-day naturalists, deists hijack their sense of right and wrong from the Christian roots from which they started. If Christian theism is undermined, this will also undermine the goodness of both atheists and deists.

Also, the deistic worldview includes a wise, good, and mighty Creator, but this Creator is aloof from the lives of human beings. He does not involve himself in the messes people get themselves into. He does not get his hands "dirty" dealing with issues of social injustice. This raises a reasonable question. If the deist has this kind of a God, then is it not reasonable to predict that the deist will also hold him or herself aloof from human problems? By our standard of a good person, aloofness is not a good posture. How does a deist answer this difficult question?

The Greek philosophy known as Epicureanism has been described as deist. Christianity is not the only idea which has produced deism. Did the Epicureans remain aloof from human problems? The answer is that Epicurus taught a kind of aloofness as the preferred style of life.[51] He told his followers that the search for pleasure was the chief good in life but that this pleasure derived not from hedonism but from living moderately, avoiding suffering, and avoiding overindulgence in worldly pleasures. He and his followers withdrew from active political life as this conflicted with the greatest good: to pursue peace of mind and the Greek virtues. This illustrates the point that the natural lifestyle of the deist is to be like his or her God—to stand aloof from human tragedy and social injustice. This does not create the kind of "good" person we have described.

Can we reasonably predict that a person who lives a life consistent

---

51 R. W. Sharples, *Stoics, Epicureans and Sceptics: An Introduction to Hellenistic Philosophy* (New York: Routledge, 1996), p. 84.

with a deistic worldview will be a better person than he or she might otherwise have been? To summarize, what we know of deism tells us that it will produce better people than naturalism, nihilism, postmodernism, or pantheism. Still, it leaves some areas of concern about absolute moral truth and compassionate involvement in helping those in need. We can note that historically, much of the good done by deists is derived from their theistic roots, not their deistic worldview.

The last set of worldviews we will analyze falls under the broader label of theism. We will look at Islamic theism, biblical theism, and deterministic Christian theism. Here is a definition:

Theism: The view that the universe is created by an omnipotent, omniscient, and omnipresent Creator who is a person and who is actively involved in human affairs.

The principal difference between deism and theism is the deity's role in the world. The theistic God is active in the world. He intervenes in supernatural ways. This world is not simply a machine that was put in motion and then proceeds naturally. There is a word for this quality of God. It is called immanence. Immanence is the property of being present and active in the world. In deism, God is transcendent but not immanent. To say that God is transcendent is to say that he is beyond, above, and outside of the world. Theism and deism agree on this quality of the Creator. Pantheism, on the other hand, does not see God as transcendent. God can be both transcendent and immanent. He can be both greater than the universe and be involved in the universe. This is the view of biblical Christian theism. We will see that one significant difference between the Islamic and the Christian worldview is in their idea of how immanent God is.

Although we will look at different theistic worldviews, they will be more similar to one another than they will be different. It is not a secret that there has been a significant amount of conflict between peoples who hold to Islamic and to Christian theism. Experience tells us that often our most bitter enemy is the one most similar to us. Yet, for at least one of these theistic systems, if its followers were to follow the tenets of its founder, this mutual enmity would come to an end. Christ commands Christians to love their enemies. This is not the case in Islam.

TEN

Islamic Theism

The first theistic worldview we will analyze is *Islamic Theism*. As already stated, Islamic theism is similar to the Christian version. However, we will see that there are significant differences as well. A Pew research study in 2020 concluded that there were roughly 1.90 billion Muslims. This comprises about 24% of the entire human population. The worldview we are now considering is fundamental for us to understand and evaluate, if for no other reason than because such a large portion of humanity holds to it.

Islam was founded by its chief prophet Muhammad (AD 571-632). Muhammad was born in Mecca, where he was part of the Quraish tribe. He claims that in 610, he was visited by the angel Gabriel while praying in a cave. Over the following years, Gabriel dictated to him the various suras, which were eventually collected to create the Qur'an, the principal scripture of Islam. He began preaching his new religion in 613. Muhammad gained very few converts in Mecca and was fiercely persecuted by his polytheistic fellow Quraishi tribesmen. He fled with most of his followers to Medina in 622 AD, an event known as the *Hijra.* In Medina, he began to make many converts and unite the various tribes there. He mounted several raids on caravans in the area, in some cases leading the raiding party himself. He agreed to the execution of more than 700 Jewish males in Medina. In 629, he led an army of 10,000 to Mecca, which he captured virtually without a fight. After this, he began a series of military campaigns across the Arab peninsula. By his death in 632, nearly all of Arabia had been conquered and converted to Islam. In the subsequent fifty years, Muslim armies under the caliphs conquered all of Persia, much of the Byzantine Empire, and nearly all of North Africa.

Having given a concise history, we must ask ourselves what the worldview of Islam is. We will principally allow the Qur'an to reveal its worldview, as we allow the Bible to define the Christian worldview. In addition, we will let the Hadith and the common understanding in the Muslim community today inform how to understand the Islamic worldview. The Hadith is a set of writings from two or three centuries after Muhammad died. They include biographical information, Qur'an interpretation, and discussions about Islamic law which preceded current sharia law. The Hadith is considered by Muslims to be inspired, but to a lesser degree than the Qur'an. Much of what Muslims believe comes from Hadith.

The Islamic worldview is sufficiently similar to the biblical one that we will start by repeating what was said earlier about the Christian worldview and explain that of Islam by distinction to it:

1. The physical world is a) real, b) created out of nothing (*ex nihilo*), and c) essentially good.

2. There exists an unseen spiritual reality that is not limited to or defined by physical reality. Human beings have a spiritual and physical aspect of their nature.

3. The creator of both the physical and spiritual realm is the God who reveals himself in the Bible.

4. God is characterized by certain qualities. He is a person. He is love. He is good. He is just. He is holy, sovereign, omniscient, omnipotent, and omnipresent.

5. Although all of God's creation is good, evil exists. Evil is the result of a rebellion by persons with a free will against the will of their Creator.

6. Because of God's justice and holiness, those who choose to rebel against him will ultimately be judged and separated from God for eternity.

7. God's love solves the solution to the problem of evil and eternal separation from God through the atoning sacrifice of Jesus Christ.

On the first three points, the worldview of Islam is identical, with the minor exception that God reveals himself principally through the Qur'an. Muhammad stated in the Qur'an that God spoke authoritatively to the Jews in the Hebrew Bible and to the Christians in what we call the

New Testament (and Muhammad calls *injil*). He called Jews and Christians "peoples of the book." However, the revelation to Muhammad in the Qur'an is Allah's final and most significant word. Regarding the authority of the New Testament, we find in Sura 5:47, "Let the people of the Gospel [i.e. Christians] judge by what Allah hath revealed therein [i.e., In the New Testament]. If any do fail to judge by (the light of) what Allah has revealed, they are (no better than) those who rebel."[52] (Note that I am using Allah and God as interchangeable words. The word for "God" in Arabic is Allah. In Muslim countries, Christians call God Allah) There are inevitable differences between what was taught by Muhammad and what is found in the New Testament. For example, the Qur'an is definite in its claim that Jesus was not crucified. It is also strident in its statements that Jesus is not God. The difference in teaching and historical information is explained by Muslims and by Muhammad by claiming the Christian scriptures have been corrupted. The evidence does not support this claim, but that is a story for a different book.[53]

With this proviso, the picture of God in Genesis chapter one is the picture of Allah in the Qur'an. Allah is one. Allah is the Creator, who created the universe out of nothing by his spoken word. In Islam, as in the Bible, the physical world is real and good. There are both spiritual and physical worlds in the Qur'an and the Bible. The world is inhabited by jinn in the Qur'an, which is much like the angels of the Bible (although generally with a more negative connotation in the case of Jinn)

When we get to point four above, Islam is similar but not identical in describing the nature of God. Islam agrees that God is holy, sovereign, omniscient, omnipotent, and omnipresent. However, the emphasis on these qualities in Islam is quite different. As we read the Qur'an, we find the qualities of Allah most strongly emphasized are his Oneness, sovereignty, and transcendence. Other attributes, such as his love, are far less stressed. In Islam, God is much more distant from humans. There is nothing like the Genesis account of an intimate relationship between God and Adam in the Qur'an. There is nothing in Islam like the closeness and the

---

52 Quotes from the Qur'an are taken from the translation by Abdullah Yusuf Ali, which is considered by many to be the most authoritative and readable of the English translations. It should be noted that Muslims believe that the Qur'an should only be read in its original Arabic and that any translation changes the meaning to an unacceptable degree.

53 John Oakes, *Reasons for Belief* (Spring, TX: IPI, 2005)

personal connection that God has with his children in Christianity. In Islam, we do not find anything remotely like the Christian teaching of the Holy Spirit living in God's people. God is distant. God is removed from direct human experience. The sovereignty of Allah is far more emphasized in Islam than in Christianity. As James Sire puts it, in Islamic theism, "God's transcendence far outweighs his immanence."[54]

In Islam, God is knowable, but only to a limited degree. Of course, this is also true in Christianity, but it is more predominant in Islam. One can talk about God's love for humans in Islam, but this is not emphasized. Instead, the biblical emphasis on God's love for his people is replaced by God's mercy in the Muslim Scripture. In the Bible, God says things such as, "Can a mother forget the baby at her breast and have no compassion on the child she has borne? Though she may forget, I will not forget you. See, I have engraved you on the palms of my hands..." (Isaiah 49:15-16). If we read the Qur'an, it is inconceivable that Allah would say something like this to Muhammad or Muslims in general.

It is not that Allah is utterly impersonal in Islam or has no closeness with his people at all, but there is a significant qualitative difference. Muslims can be defensive about this. They will quote from Sura 50:16, "We are nearer to him than (his) jugular vein." However, if we look at this line in its context, it reveals something different from the biblical quality of a personal relationship with his people. Sura 50:16-17 says, "It was We who created man, and We know what dark suggestions his soul makes to him: for We are nearer to him than (his) jugular vein. Behold, two (guardian angels) appointed to learn (his doings) learn (and note them)." Here we see that the closeness described has an ominous tone. It is about Allah checking up on his people to know if they are doing evil. There is no intimacy here!

Another statement Muslims use to "prove" that Allah is as close to us in Islam as he is in Christianity is Sura 2:186. As before, when we look at the context, it does not reveal intimacy. "When my servants ask thee concerning Me, I am indeed close (to them): I listen to the prayer of every suppliant when he calleth on Me: Let them also, with a will, listen to My call, and believe in me." In other words, I am close to them, but only if they listen to me and obey me.

And what about point five in the description of the Christian world-

---

53 James W. Sire, *The Universe Nest Door* (Downer's Grove, Il: InterVarsity, 2020), p. 239.

view above? "Although all God's creation is good, evil exists. Evil is the result of rebellion by persons with free will against the will of their Creator." Here, as with point four, Islam is similar but definitely not the same. Both theisms agree that evil is real and that it is the result of the actions of human beings. But there is a big difference here. It is questionable if free will is even a concept in the Qur'an. Islam can be described as a deterministic religion. We can talk about Islamic Determinism. By this is meant that in Islam, everything which happens is predetermined by Allah. Islam has a closed, not an open, theology. The Christian world is an open one. In both the Old and the New Testaments, one can find innumerable examples of God deciding what to do based on the desires of human beings. The scene in Genesis 18:16-33, in which God takes input from Abraham on the fate of Sodom, is perhaps the most famous example, but there are many more. In the Christian universe, God is sovereign. True, but in the biblical world, what happens is determined by the Creator, but also by human beings, with their desires and their sovereign wills taken into account. In Christianity, it is God's sovereign will to give his creatures sovereign will within their own sphere. In Christianity, God respects his sovereign created persons—giving them the space to act according to their own will and even respecting them and allowing himself to be influenced by their desires.

There is nothing like this in Islam! A major doctrine in Islam is the idea of *Qadr*. The word can be translated as power, but it has a strong connotation of Determinism. This Determinism is found in the Qur'an but also in the religion as reflected in modern practice. We see in the Qur'an that Allah has full knowledge of what has happened and what will happen, but this "knowledge" implies control, not mere awareness. We can read in Sura 57:22-23, "No misfortune can happen on earth or in your souls but is recorded in a decree before We bring it into existence: This is truly easy for Allah. In order that ye may not despair over the matters that pass you by, nor exult over favours bestowed upon you." A key word here is "decree." A man may think that random things happen or that their decisions determine their future, but Allah tells us that everything is by his decree. We will see below that there is a flavor of Christianity similar to Islamic Determinism. We will be describing Christian Determinism which has been called Calvinism. Calvinists have much to say about God's decrees.

I am not just taking a single passage in the Qur'an out of context here. The tone of the entire Qur'an supports this idea of Determinism, and

Muslims are aware of this. To engage in conversation with a Muslim is to hear repeated again and again the word *"inshallah."* It is God's will. Islam is a fatalistic religion. Of course, Christians say "it is God's will" as well, but the tone is quite different. We say that God is in control, but biblically, we know that he is not in complete control. In his paradigmatic prayer, Jesus said to his Father, "Your will be done." In other words, God's will is not always done, but we pray it will be done. In July 1990, there was a tragic death of more than one thousand four hundred pilgrims in Mecca at the *hadj.* When asked about the tragedy, King Fahd said, "It was God's will, which is above everything... It was fate."[55] The Muslim world did not bat an eyelash at this statement. A Christian (hopefully) would never say such a thing about a tragic loss of life.

Remember that in Islam, the qualities of God most highly emphasized are his Oneness, sovereignty, and transcendence. In the Qur'an, Allah has full knowledge of all that happens, but this knowledge amounts to predetermining what happens. To quote Sura 6:59, "Not a leaf doth fall but with his knowledge: there is not a grain in the darkness (or depths) of the earth, nor anything fresh or dry (green or withered) but is (inscribed) in a record clear (to those who can read)."

In Islam, Allah determines everything: even who will choose to follow him and those who will be in Paradise or Hell. In Sura 2:142, Muhammad tells us about Allah that "He guideth whom He will to a Way that is straight." Also, in Sura 6:39, "Those who reject Our Signs are deaf and dumb—in the midst of darkness profound: whom Allah willeth, He leaveth to wander: whom He willeth, He placeth on the way that is straight." There is no equivalent passage in the Christian Scriptures. Other passages in the Qur'an that lay out Islamic predestination include 6:25, 6:35, and 6:125.

On point #6 above, Islam and Christianity agree, "Because of God's justice and his holiness, those who choose to rebel against him will ultimately be judged and separated from God for eternity." But on point #7, there is a significant divergence. "God's love solves the solution to the problem of evil and eternal separation from God through the atoning sacrifice of Jesus Christ." Both theisms agree on the nature of the problem of evil, but they diverge widely on the solution. Let us be reminded that in Islam, the operative word is mercy, whereas, in Christianity and Judaism, it is love.

---

53 *New York Times,* July 4, 1990.

There is nothing in Islam similar to the biblical doctrine of salvation. There is no justification. There is no assurance of Paradise in Islam. Most importantly, there is nothing remotely like redemption. There is a kind of grace in Islam, but that grace is a carrot and a stick. In Islam, the only sure ticket to Paradise is martyrdom for the cause of Islam. The only unforgivable sin in Islam is *shirk*, which is the association of other gods (idols) with Allah. If there is salvation in the Qur'an, it is through what Christians call works salvation. We read in the Qur'an, in Sura 11:114, "for those things that are good remove those that are evil." In Sura 7:43, we hear Allah declaring, "Behold the Garden before you! Ye have been made its inheritors for your deeds (of righteousness)." In Sura 2:271, those who submit to the will of Allah are told that their acts of charity will "remove from you some of your (stains of) evil." The devoted Muslim is perpetually in need of Allah's mercy. There is no final assurance of Paradise. Colin Chapman, a professor of Islamic studies at Beirut University, said about the Muslims, "This understanding of forgiveness, however, leaves us open to a frightening uncertainty since we can never have any assurance about God's verdict for each individual on the day of judgment."[56]

In Christian theism, God reaches down and lifts up his created persons. God comes near to us in the most striking of ways in his Son. In Islamic theism, people must constantly lift themselves up to approach a distant and nearly unknowable God.

The Christian and the Islamic worldview are similar in their description of the final state of humans. Both propose an eternal destiny, either in heaven/Paradise or hell. Much has been made of the supposed worldliness of heaven as presented in the Qur'an. This charge is not without merit. For example, in Sura 37:40-49 we read, "The true servants of Allah will be well provided for, feasting on fruit and honored in gardens of delight. Reclining face to face upon soft couches, they shall be served with a goblet filled at a gushing fountain... delicious to those who drink it. They shall sit with bashful, dark-eyed virgins, chaste as the sheltered eggs of ostriches."

The description of Paradise in the Qur'an is geared toward men, not women. In fairness, it is debatable how true this charge of Allah using worldly inducement to good deeds is. Christians do not take the

54 Colin Chapman, *The Cross and the Crescent: Responding to the Challenges of Islam* (Downers Grove, IL: InterVarsity, 2003), p. 259-260.

description of heaven in Revelation in Revelation 21 literally, and perhaps Muslims do the same with their Scripture. Indeed, devout Muslim women expect their final place with Allah to be similar to that of men. The reader can decide how justified the charge of worldly inducement to good deeds is in the Qur'an.

To summarize, in Islamic theism, salvation is earned through the efforts of those pre-selected by Allah to inhabit a relatively sensual paradise. In Christian theism, salvation is granted by the grace of a loving God to those who, through faith and repentance, accept that love. I will now proceed to analyze whether Islam provides a "good" view of the world.

Is it True?

Is Islamic theism true in that what it tells us about the world is consistent with what we can observe? The answer to this question is found primarily in the first three points, as outlined above. The answer is yes! Islamic theism proposes a single Creator/God who is essentially good and created the universe. Therefore, the universe we observe ought to be created and ought to obey a single set of unchanging laws of nature. All of this is confirmed by human experience and by scientific observation. The universe is indeed created, as cosmology informs us, and it is ordered and governed by a single set of universal laws. It is not chaotic but inherently predictable. If it is evil, such evil is not found in the physical creation.

Islam also explains evil in a way that is more or less consistent with human experience. Islamic theism correctly tells us that evil is real. It is not an illusion. It is difficult to square a good God with a universe that includes sin. But Islam gives us a somewhat surprising but believable explanation of the source of evil. This explanation is similar to but different from that provided by its cousin, Christian theism. In Islam, the sovereign God, in his great wisdom, decreed that people would be capable of doing both good and evil. He did this to display his providence and his mercy.

Is it Right?

What about the answers an Islamic worldview provides to the most important human questions?

Why am I here?
What is my purpose?

How did I get here?
What is my value?
What is a human being?
What is the right thing to do?
Is or will there be ultimate justice?
What is the nature of ultimate reality?
What happens to me when I die?

My answer to this question is that the Islamic version of theism does relatively well here—second only to Christian theism. In Islam, humans have great value. They are the highest of God's creation—even higher than the angels (or the jinn in Islam). In the Islamic worldview, mankind also has a purpose: to submit to Allah and glorify him.

However, the Islamic worldview falls short of Christian theism in assigning value and purpose to human beings. The Christian description of God's relationship with humanity is that we are His treasured possession. It is hard to see that in the Qur'an, which describes a more impersonal and distant relationship. In the Bible, humans are described as the apple of God's eye (Psalm 17:8). We have already seen suras in the Qur'an, which represents the closeness of Allah to people more like a boss checking up on his workers than a mother caring for her children. We experience mercy, not love. A word in the Old Testament that describes how God values his people is *hesed*. The term is translated as loyal love, unfailing love, and kindness. It is the kind of love that is shared in the family. This familial closeness of God to his people is not found in the Qur'an.

As for purpose, the Islamic worldview does see an excellent purpose for humans as they submit their will to Allah, glorifying him and being glorified in return. The same can be said for Christian theism. Many in Christianity see their primary purpose as giving glory to God. But other Christians believe that the ultimate purpose for humans is to love God, to be loved by him, and to love one another. This is the case when we look at the Genesis creation account. We will not settle this debate here, but the point is that Christian theism provides a better answer to the purpose than its closest rival. The very doctrine of the trinity is about God's relational nature. Great purpose in Islamic theism—yes! Still greater purpose, though, in Christian theism.

Value and purpose are "better" in Christianity than in Islamic theism.

The counterargument a Muslim might make is that the Qur'an is true and the biblical description is not accurate—the Christian worldview is more like pie-in-the-sky. The Bible lowers God to become too much like us, and therefore it lessens God's glory. The idea of God taking on the form of a human degrades God. Perhaps the Qur'an is true, and the Bible is false on this question. If this were so, it would reflect not so much on which gives better answers but on the first point, which is that a "good" worldview is one which is true. This raises the question of whose Scripture is more reliable—a matter of apologetics. This volume is not a book of evidential apologetics. Still, it is worth pointing out that the reliability of the Bible is supported by dozens of historically fulfilled prophecies, reliable history, and confirmed miracles, especially the resurrection of Christ. The Qur'an has none of these things. If it is confirmed at all, it is self-confirmed. The clear and undeniable evidence for the reliability of the Bible tends to support the conclusion that Christian theism is right on matters of value and purpose.

There are other items in our list of essential questions that a worldview must provide consistent, believable, and satisfactory answers to. This includes How did I get here? What is a human being? What is the right thing to do? Will there be ultimate justice? What is the nature of ultimate reality? What happens to me when I die? On these questions, Islamic theism provides answers very similar to Christian theism. And they are great answers. A human being is a self-aware person created in the image of God. A single Creator/God determines ultimate reality. The moral systems of the two theisms have more in common than different, and they establish solid grounds for humans to know the right thing to do. Both theisms propose that justice is not just a word—that God will bring justice to the righteous and the wicked and that good will prevail. Both envision that life in our mortal bodies is not the end, providing a vision for the possibility of a more extraordinary life with God in the future.

Is it Better?

On the questions of being true and providing good answers, Islamic theism does very well—only eclipsed by Christian theism. On the question of which worldview produces a better person, we will see that the Islamic worldview does not fare as well. The question is this: from what we know of Islamic theism, can we conclude that those who consistently apply it to their lives will be the most self-controlled, least selfish, most honest, peace-loving, and compassionate person possible? The answer is no, for a few reasons.

On the positive side, one of the five pillars of Islam is almsgiving. Self-sacrifice is baked into Islam, and that is a good thing. According to the Qur'an, the purpose of the alms is to meet the needs of the less fortunate. This is an outstanding characteristic. The command to help the needy makes Muslims better than they might otherwise have been. One major drawback, however, is that Islamic law dictates that such alms are only used to help fellow Muslims. I once challenged a Muslim on this question. He retorts that Muslims are allowed to help non-Muslims, but only if all the needs in the Muslim community are met. The problem with this is that there will always be needs in the Muslim community. Because of this pillar of faith, the benevolent needs of Muslim countries and peoples tend to be met by their fellow Muslims, which is good. However, it is rare indeed to find Muslim charities helping non-Muslims. This is almost unheard of. According to our analysis of whether Islamic theism makes for a better person than he or she might otherwise have been, this is a mixed bag. There is no question that Christian theism is superior, as we will discuss below.

Then there is the issue of whether Islamic theism will likely produce peace-loving and compassionate people. Can we reasonably conclude from what is taught in the Qur'an and Hadith and from what is demonstrated in the life of Muhammad that Muslims will be open-minded and tolerant, and will they behave peacefully toward people with different views? The answer to this question is a fairly strong no. From its inception, Islam took a war-like posture. Muhammad set an example in this area by leading armies and conquering foes. Islam is, by its very nature, militant. It is not peace-loving. Individual Muslims may be lovers of peace, but their worldview does not strongly support this. Entire books in Hadith are devoted to military tactics. The concept of *jihad* has been debated. Some have even called jihad a sixth pillar of Islam. There is a wide range of interpretations of this word, which means struggle. For many, it is only about the spiritual, internal struggle to be good. For others, it is about the struggle to establish Islamic law everywhere on the earth by all possible means. Which of these is most consistent with the Qur'an and Hadith?

I mentioned earlier a debate that the organization I am president of put on with an atheist. Another debate we sponsored at Elmhurst College

in Chicago was on the following premise: Judaism, Christianity, and Islam: Which is the True Legacy of Abraham? Speaking for Islam was Imam
Shabir Ally. Speaking for Judaism was Rabbi Shmuley Boteach. Speaking
for Christianity, again, was my friend Douglas Jacoby. One stark distinction was raised in the debate. Both Ally and Boteach challenged Jacoby
on this: Christianity is a religion of pacifism. The founder of Christianity preached love of the enemy. Both opponents in the debate challenged
Christianity on this point. Let us be clear on this. Much evil had been done
in the name of Christianity. The crusades come to mind, but others can
be enumerated. They are a dark stain on the religion. But one thing that
no one will debate is this: Jesus preached a gospel of love, including love
for our enemies. Jesus was not called the Prince of Peace for nothing. He
would not have condoned the Crusades!

Such is not the case with Islam. For example, in Sura 2:216-218 we
read, "Warfare is prescribed for you, though you dislike it... Behold, those
who believe, emigrate, and undertake jihad, these have hope of the mercy of Allah." Wherever the debate over the nature of Islamic *jihad* ends
up, one thing we can be sure of, Muhammad was not a prophet of peace,
and his concept of *jihad* included warfare. Of course, many Muslims abhor warfare, but the question is whether their religion naturally promotes
this stance. This is a significant negative for whether Islamic theism produces better people.

Do Muslims tend to be tolerant people? Are they capable of disagreeing with people but still respecting them? Individually, many of them are.
Once they reach majority status in society, are Muslims kind to and in-
clusive of outsiders? If not, why not? Historically, Islam has had a relatively tolerant approach to people of the book—Jews and Christians. Still,
when it comes to pagans and idolaters, the policy has been anything but
peaceful and tolerant. For example, we can read in Sura 9:5, "For when
the forbidden months are past, then fight and slay the Pagans wherever
ye find them, beleaguer them, and lie in wait for them in every stratagem
(of war). But if they repent, establish regular prayers, and practice regular
charity, then open the way for them." Even to "people of the book," the
Qur'an is not as tolerant as one might hope. For example, there is Sura
9:29-30. "Fight those who believe not in Allah, nor the last day... (even if
they are) of the People of the Book, until they pay the *jizyah* [the head tax
for all non-Muslims] with willing submission, and feel subdued... Allah's

curse be on them."

Hell is referenced in the Qur'an several hundred times. In more than 90% of these cases, people are warned of hell, not for moral reasons or sin, but for disagreeing with Muhammad. Islam is not a religion that accepts dissent readily. Its natural tendency is to create a closed society. Islam is an inherently political religion, one of whose goals is to create an Islamic state. This is not a positive for the question of whether Islamic theism will produce a "better" person than those who live their lives consistent with other worldviews.

ELEVEN

Christian Theism

Is Christian theism a good worldview? Is it true, is it right, and is it better? The reader can probably guess where this is going, but many details remain to be hashed out. The Christian worldview was already described in chapter three. Here is our summary, taken from the first four chapters of Genesis:

1. The physical world is a. real b. created out of nothing (*ex nihilo*), and c. essentially good.

2. There exists an unseen spiritual reality that is not limited to or defined by physical reality. Human beings have a spiritual and physical aspect of their nature.

3. The creator of the physical and spiritual realms is the God who reveals himself in the Bible.

4. God is characterized by certain qualities. He is a person. He is love. He is good. He is just. He is holy, sovereign, omniscient, omnipotent, and omnipresent.

5. Although all of God's creation is good, evil exists. Evil is the result of a rebellion by persons with a free will against the will of their Creator.

6. Because of God's justice and holiness, those who choose to rebel against him will ultimately be judged and separated from God for eternity.

7. God's love solves the solution to the problem of evil and eternal separation from God through the atoning sacrifice of Jesus Christ.

In this chapter, we will ask whether this worldview is true, right, and better than its competitors.

Is It True?

Is this description of the world consistent with what we can induce about the world from experience, and is it compatible with what human reason tells us must be true? The answer will be a resounding yes.

First, let us consider cosmology. Scientific observation has revealed a world governed by a single set of laws of nature. From what we can tell, these laws are consistent throughout time and space. It also informs us that the universe came into existence in a moment, literally out of nothing. As the Hebrew writer put it, *"so that what is seen was not made our of what is visible."* (Hebrews 11:3). These facts imply that the physical universe was created from nothing by a single, all-powerful, unchanging Creator. Add to this the fact that the universe is wonderfully made. As physicists put it, it is finely tuned in an unimaginably precise way. Creation produces an overwhelming sense of order, beauty, and design. This could only be the result of personal intelligence. Everything we know from science tells us that the universe we live in was specifically designed to allow for the existence of advanced life forms.[57] This hints at the idea (but does not prove) that the universe itself has a purpose. That purpose is so that a certain kind of advanced life-form, namely humans, can exist. These facts are consistent with monotheism.

Before the scientific revolution, Christians generally believed that the earth was the center of the universe. They did so, falsely, on the presumption that humans were the center of the universe, but also because of the obvious observation that heavenly objects seem to circle the earth. But then Copernicus proposed, and Galileo proved decisively that the earth is not at the center. We exist on one of several relatively small planets, circling (actually on ellipti-

Henrietta Swan Leavitt (1868-1921)

cal orbits) a much larger sun. Still, in the seventeenth century, we thought we were close to the center. But by the nineteenth century, it had become apparent that our sun was just one of millions of stars at vast and varying distances in a humungous galaxy. We were a small planet on a fairly average star amongst millions of other stars. Then with the work of Henrietta Swan Leavitt and Edwin Hubble in the 1920s, we discovered that nearly

---

57 For much more on this, see John Oakes, *Is There a God* (Spring, TX: IPI, 200.

all the visible stars are part of one particular galaxy that we call the Milky Way but that there are billions of other galaxies. Our little reality on the earth had shrunk to mind-numbing insignificance. We were much smaller than the Whos down in Whoville.

By the early twentieth century, the idea that humans occupy a central place in the universe appeared to have been disproved. All this changed as cosmologists investigated the details of the universe-creating event. A detailed look at the big bang model led to the discovery that almost every parameter that governs how the universe works is "finely tuned," Some of these parameters, such as the force of gravity, are finely tuned to phenomenal precision. The universe appears well-tuned so that advanced life forms can exist. If we assume that a universe can be created—a big assumption—the probability that any randomly-generated universe could support advanced life forms is infinitesimally tiny. It is hard to overstate how low this probability is. This led to the Strong Anthropic Principle, which proposes that the only reasonable way to explain why the universe has the properties it has was that it was designed so that advanced, intelligent life forms can live in it and understand how it works. We are back at the center of creation, not physically, but metaphorically. The universe is purposeful. It gives every appearance that it exists so that we can exist. There is excellent cosmological truth in the Christian worldview.

But as was inferred earlier, one statement in Genesis raises challenging questions about the trueness of Christian theism. This is a theological, not a cosmological, problem. In Genesis 1:31, we read, "God saw all that he had made, and it was very good." This raises two questions that can challenge the trueness of Christian theism.

1. We can agree that nature, generally, is good, but what about natural disasters such as earthquakes, hurricanes, and tsunamis, and the subsequent suffering? And what about infectious diseases, congenital disabilities, and other seemingly unnecessary sufferings? How can these exist in a "very good" world governed by a benevolent, omnipotent God?

2. What about the evil in the world? If everything was created so good, why do we have things like genocide, murder, drug addiction, and all kinds of evil? How can a perfect world include evil? Did God create evil?

We will consider a biblical answer to both of these questions. At the same time, we will query how other worldviews answer the same questions, some of which we have already done. We will take on these questions in reverse order. First, we will ask why evil exists in a world that was created all good.

First of all, is evil real? Everyone should consider this problem. However, speaking for myself, when I see jetliners being purposefully crashed into the World Trade Center when I see genocide committed on the Jews, the Armenians, and the Cambodian people, I see evil. When I hear of men sexually abusing minor children, I believe sin is real. On a personal level, when I see one of my wife's best friend's daughter shot in the head by her drug-dealing boyfriend, with her two-year-old child in the room, I say that is evil. To deny the reality of evil is to deny reality itself.

How can a world created very good and governed by an all-powerful and loving God allow such evil? If God is truly sovereign—if he is in control, as they say—how can evil exist? Is he not powerful enough to prevent evil? Is he not as loving as we thought? This is a difficult question.

What is the answer from other worldviews? To the naturalist, evil is not real. Everything real is measurable. Morality is not quantifiable. Therefore, there is no absolute right and wrong, no moral truth or evil. Actions can be unethical but not immoral. Materialism does not solve the problem of evil. Ignoring something does not make it go away. For the pantheist, there is only one reality, and that reality is not evil. Like the lower physical realities, evil is, in essence, an illusion. It is *maya*. Again, this does not solve the problem of evil. It also provides relatively less motivation for fighting evil if it is only illusory. For the dualist, good and evil are in an endless struggle, and neither will win out. For the determinist Islamic theist, God hates evil, but he is also the cause of evil. This is confusing. It does not make sense. None of the competing worldviews offer a solution to the problem of evil that is either helpful or consistent with reality.

As difficult as the Christian answer to the question of evil is to understand and accept, it is the only one that works. First of all, the biblical worldview accepts that evil is real. It does not ignore reality. Second, Christian theism can give a rational, if complex, answer to the question of evil. God is love. Love always offers a choice. We cannot force anyone to love us. God wants to love us, and God wants us to love him, and he wants us to love one another. God wanted to give and receive love, so he created persons who have free will because this is the only kind of person who can give and receive love. And like was said earlier, free will implies choice, and that choice had to be real. Adam and Eve were given everything they could possibly need, but they were also given the opportunity, if they so choose, to rebel against their loving Creator and eat from the tree of the knowledge of good and evil. God forbade it for them because it was bad for them, yet he left them to choose. The fruit was attractive. If it had not been, there would have been no real choice. And thus, evil came into the world.

Genesis 3-11 is the story of what happens when humans choose to rebel against God and to do evil. It leads to a rapid downhill spiral into greater and greater evil. We, too, have a choice. But apparently, we have inherited a propensity to choose evil. The sin and rebellion of Adam led to evil in the world, and all of us who rebel against our Creator are guilty of adding to the problem of evil. Christianity is "true" on the question of evil.

But what about suffering? Does Christian theism provide an accurate and consistent explanation of human suffering? For the sake of argument, let us assume that the Christian explanation of evil given above is proper. If so, then naturally, much of the suffering in the world is the direct result of people rebelling against God and doing evil things. So much suffering results from greed, selfishness, arrogance, lust, the desire for control, deceit, and other forms of evil. When Christian theism correctly explains the cause of evil, it also explains the cause of much—perhaps even most of the suffering in the world. This cause-and-effect relationship between sin and suffering is described in Exodus 20:5, in which the Jews are told that God allows punishment for the parents' sin down to the fourth generation. We, humans, are well aware of the generational negative effects of sin—most suffering results from rebellion against a loving God who gives choices to those he loves.

However, even the most superficial observation of the world tells us that not all suffering results from someone's sin. In John 9:1-34 there is a story of a man born blind. The Jews asked Jesus the cause of the man's blindness. To them, there were two options. Either the parents sinned, causing the blindness, or perhaps the son's sin caused him to be blind. Never mind that he was born blind, meaning he would have had to have sinned while in his mother's womb. Jesus corrected the worldview error of the Jews. Not all suffering is the result of someone's sin. In this case, Jesus told them that *"this happened so that the works of God might be displayed in him."* (John 9:3). With rare exceptions, blindness is not caused by the evil acts of human beings. A genetic defect, infectious disease, or accidental injury can cause it. It seems irrational to blame hurricanes, tornadoes, earthquakes, and tsunamis on human sin. Although human-caused climate change might have some effect on wildfires and other weather-born disasters, the fact is that at least some of such disasters are "natural." Sin does not cause natural things to happen. They happen naturally.

If Christian theism is true and God is omnipotent, omniscient, and omnipresent, how can Christian theism explain natural disasters? This is not an easy question, but, as with the question of evil, Christian theism offers a rational answer consistent with the Christian idea of a good and powerful God. For example, earthquakes and tsunamis are the natural results of a wonderfully created world in which planets have plate tectonics. Plate tectonics is like a massive mineral-recycling system. If it were not for plate tectonics, we would not have fertile soil. Nor would we have an atmosphere. Plate tectonics is a good thing in the big picture. Unless someone can propose a "better" set of physical laws of the universe, which create livable environments with no plate tectonics, I will not charge the Creator with doing a lousy job. The same goes for tragic weather events such as hurricanes. With thermal energy reaching the planet in the form of light from a distant star (the results of a wonderfully designed energy-providing system), and with a round planet, that energy must be distributed efficiently. Otherwise, life could not be supported on round planets, the only kind there is. Weather is the Creator's way of spreading solar energy relatively evenly across a spherical world. Again, this is a good thing, and the fact that some suffering occurs with the effects of weather does not diminish the goodness of God.

What about genetic diseases or infectious diseases? Why would a reasonable, benevolent, and omnipotent God create these things? This is a more difficult question, but one thing we can say for sure is that without bacteria, the atmosphere would have no oxygen or nitrogen. Genetic mutation is an absolute requirement for species to evolve. If we look deeply into the created universe, we find that it is the best possible world, and the goodness of God is maintained.

Besides, the idea that suffering and death disprove God's love is false. In the biblical world of Christian theism, God's deep compassion for those suffering is demonstrated by the Son of God, Jesus Christ (John 11:35, Matthew 9:36, for example). Having said this, suffering is not inherently evil. Physical pain is required to prevent death. Arguably, there is no joy without sorrow. Although most of us do not seek suffering, one does not have to be a Christian to know that *"suffering produces perseverance, perseverance, character, and character hope."* (Romans 5:3-4) Suffering is not evil, and its existence does not disprove the presence of a powerful and benevolent God. We will have more to say about the Christian response to suffering below.

What about other worldviews? Do they provide a more consistent explanation of suffering? On the question of suffering, pantheism informs us that it is ultimately not real. It is *maya*—an illusion. This is not a satisfactory answer to the question of suffering. If a Buddhist or Hindu were consistent, they would not mind being punched in the nose, as suffering is an illusion. But we know that it is no illusion. Materialism tells us that suffering is meaningless—the result of random events governed by impersonal laws of the universe. If that were true, it would be depressing at best. Yet, human experience tells us that even atheists find meaning in the suffering that they endure. "It made me a better person." Postmodernism produces no coherent explanation of suffering at all. Polytheism tells us it is the result of the acts of capricious gods or perhaps due to humans not avoiding certain taboos. Islam gives an overly simplistic answer that all, including suffering, is God's will. Although the existence of evil and suffering raises natural questions about the truthfulness of the Christian worldview, in the final analysis, I conclude that everything I know to be true from experience and rational inference from that experience tells me that the Christian worldview is true. It is consistent with what we can observe in the universe, including human suffering.

Is It Right?

Christian theism is true, but does it provide believable, satisfactory answers to the questions that every human being needs to be answered? Let us see. Here is our proposed list of critical human questions:

Why am I here?
What is my purpose
How did I get here?

What is my value?
What is a human being?
What is the right thing to do?
Is or will there be ultimate justice?
What is the nature of ultimate reality?
What happens to me when I die?

Why am I here? What, if any, is my purpose? The Christian answer is two-fold. First and most importantly, we are here because of love. We exist because, as a parent, God wants to give and receive love, and he wants his beloved children to give and receive love amongst each other. Like the Beatles said, "All you need is love." Of course, this is not completely true. We also need food, water, shelter, and security, but without love, these things do not produce meaning and purpose. What a beautiful answer to the question of why we are here! It is about love.

Another biblical reason that humans exist is so that they can give glory to their Creator/God. Like David said, *"The heavens declare the glory of God."* (Psalm 19:1). No truer words were ever uttered. But as David also said, we are *"fearfully and wonderfully made."* (Psalm 139:14). By their very nature, humans give glory to God. A human living in harmony with God and with his or her fellow humans gives God the most significant possible glory. It is a beautiful thing. Does God want to be glorified because he is a narcissist? Is it because he wants everyone to know how great he is and how insignificant we are? Perhaps we will have the opportunity to confront God with this question one day. Speaking for myself, I do not plan on doing so. As God is glorified, so is his highest creation celebrated as well. A second purpose for us as human beings is to become like God and thereby glorify him.

Speaking of human dignity, what about the question of what is a human being? Are we mere servants created to serve the gods? Are we a very complex assembly of chemical compounds, produced by random events over time, set in motion by autonomically-produced nerve impulses? Are we a drop of the universal Oneness, destined to be reabsorbed into this Oneness? The human soul demands an answer to this question. The Christian response to this essential question is that we are the pinnacle of God's creatures, created in his image. We are the *imago dei*. We are the why of the universe. We are purposeful, eternal, creative persons designed to give and receive love and to give glory to the all-powerful and all-loving God. What a great answer to the fundamental question of who we are! No religion or philosophy of human origin has conceived of such a wonderful thing.

Then there is the question of value. Here the Christian answer stands in stark contrast to other worldviews, including Islamic theism. As we have already seen, we are the apple of God's eye. To our Creator, we are infinitely valuable. Because we are created in God's image, humans inherently know the truth of this statement. If someone were to offer you one hundred million dollars to have your left hand removed, you would not take them up on the offer. The way Jesus rhetorically put it, "What good is it for someone to gain the whole world, and yet lose or forfeit their very self?" It would not be easy to calculate the amount of money required to buy all the property in the world, but surely it would be in the hundreds of trillions of dollars. The Christian answer to the question of value is that each of us is more valuable than hundreds of trillions of dollars. The fact is that all of us, including our atheist and pantheist friends, know that this is true. Maybe Christian theism is wrong on this question, but humans somehow know that it is true. What a great answer the Christian worldview gives to this most important question of value.

What is the right thing to do? Every human, including those who do not admit that absolute moral truth is objective, wants to know what is the right thing to do. The Christian response is that the right thing to do is to listen to the Word of God in the Bible and live according to its moral precepts, both in the things we morally ought to do and in the things we morally ought not to do. Not every question of what we ought to do or not to do is answered in black and white in the Scriptures of Christianity. For other situations, the Bible gives principles for deciding what is good, better, or best. In a world of moral relativism, the Bible offers moral certainty where it is needed and moral and ethical wisdom in the grey areas of life. This is an excellent answer to the question. As humans, we may not agree with all that God has spoken in the Bible on moral questions. Some will always disagree with the Biblical mandates. Humble and wise people understand that their ideas about right and wrong are subject to error. It is wonderful to have certainty on moral issues, especially if, as Christian theism claims, the Bible contains absolute moral truth.

One question some have is how does God decide right and wrong? It has been my experience that the things we are told in the Bible not to do are the things which lead to the most significant degree of happiness and fulfillment for ourselves and other people. The things we are told not to do are the things that lead to unnecessary suffering and degradation. Readers will decide for themselves, but my experience is that when I have disagreed with biblical wisdom on various points, time reveals the wisdom of biblical commandments related to moral behavior. Biblical commands and principles which relate to what is right and what is wrong work.

What about justice? In the final analysis, is the universe a place of justice? Will what is right and what is true prevail in the end? Will the abuser, the greedy, and the arrogant be called to account for their wicked abuse of the weak? The biblical worldview is that they will. There will be a final reckoning. That reckoning will be done by the one true and just God. The present world is often unfair because it is occupied by sinners who have rejected God's will for their lives, but if the Christian worldview is true, then the answer is yes. Justice will be done in the end.

Another question that humans throughout history have asked is regarding the final disposition of ourselves. When we die, do we cease to exist as persons, or is there some existence after our mortal bodies cease to function? If so, what is this life-after-death experience like? The history of religion informs us that, for some reason, humans everywhere and at all times have had a sense that this life is not all there is. Perhaps this is just wishful thinking, but the prevalence of belief in life after death may be pointing to inherent knowledge held by those made in the image of God. The Bible offers a definite answer to the question of life after death. *"Multitudes who sleep in the dust of the earth will awake: some to everlasting life, others to shame and everlasting contempt."* (Daniel 12:2). Christians debate whether passages about those who experience the second death (Revelation 21:8) imply they receive eternal punishment or whether they imply a punishment for a time, with permanent implications, followed by annihilation. The question will not be settled here. The biblical response to this question, which may be the most deeply sought answer, is that those who, through faith, seek a relationship with God will be with him in intimate fellowship for eternity. At the same time, those who choose not to inherit the kingdom of God will be kept out of fellowship with God eternally. Whether this answer is a "good" one depends on whether it is true, of course, but it also depends on the kind of life the one receiving the answer is living. Let us assume that the Bible is a source of truth (and everything we have seen in this chapter says it is). If so, then for the one who trusts fully in the Christian God, this is the best imaginable news. What a great answer to this essential question.

The last question we will consider that humans seek an answer to is this: Does human history has any meaning or ultimate direction or is history merely a record of random, human-caused events? Are we going anywhere? Whether we look in the short term or take a longer view, it is not at all clear from current events or from human history that humanity is going in a good direction. During the Enlightenment, philosophers proposed that, through the application of reason, people would gradually improve the lot of humanity, finally approaching an ideal state. With the discovery of science, and its ability to improve the human condition, the future of humanity seemed bright. But then, the dual catastrophes of the two World Wars, the creation of doomsday weapons, and the simple reality of the evil inherent in human beings destroyed this hope.

Is history going somewhere? Something inside us tells us that it is, yet our empirical experience tells us something different. The answer provided by Christian theism is clear. Human history is a story. It has a great beginning, a discouraging middle, and a perfect ending. It is the story of the kingdom of God. It is the story of God creating everything very good, with his crowning creation being made in his image. It is the story of humans, given free will but choosing to rebel. Mankind lost their intimate relationship with God. It is the story of the ever-greater degradation of men and women in rebellion against their Creator. But it is also the story of God choosing a man of faith. His name was Abraham. It is the story of God using Abraham and his faith to create a chosen people, to give them a land, a law, prophets, and an inspired Scripture. All of this points toward the most significant moment in history, when God brought to culmination his plan to restore humanity to the garden. God became like man so that man could become like God. We are now in the last era of history before God brings it to its final culmination, when heaven and earth will come together in the final kingdom of God. Biblical theism has a great answer to the question of where history is taking us.

Is it Better?

Is biblical theism better? Will a reasonable person be able to infer from what we know of Christian theism that a life lived consistently with this worldview will be better than one lived by an alternative worldview? Will a life lived in imitation of Jesus of Nazareth produce a person who is humble, generous, courageous, diligent, self-controlled, honest, self-sacrificing, loving, and peace-loving? On this question, the Christian worldview is triumphant. No other worldview comes close.

Let it be noted, however, that much evil has been done in the name of Christ. There is no use pretending differently. I attended a debate a few years ago in San Diego between Rabbi David Wolpe and arch-atheist Christopher Hitchens. The premise was whether religion, broadly, is a positive for humanity. In the debate, Hitchens pointed out that religious believers did a majority of the evil acts done in history, and many of these were done in the name of religion. Wolpe, a Jew, certainly did not duck this undeniable fact. But his reply was a good one. To paraphrase, he said, "True, but at least when a follower of God does an evil thing, they are violating a moral law from a God that they claim to believe in." In other words, theists have indeed done much evil, but at least we can say that theists hold to a truth that informs them that such actions are evil. Besides, the premise of the question of whether a worldview, logically, will make a person better is that they live a life generally consistent with that worldview. Those who sent believers on the Crusades have much answering to give to God on Judgment Day.

Undoubtedly, those who call themselves Christians have a lot to answer for. However, let us consider what the world owes to those who have accepted the Christian worldview. First off, it is Christianity that gave us science. This is a historical fact. Christian theologians such as Roger Bacon began with Christian monotheism to infer that there ought to exist a single set of unchanging laws of the universe and that those laws ought to be mathematical and discernable to humans. And thus, the scientific revolution was begun. Only monotheism could ever have produced science. Dualism and polytheism certainly could not. Neither could pantheism have produced the scientific method, as it proposes that physical things should not be paid attention to. Naturalism could not create science, as naturalism is the result of science.

Then there is the question of slavery. Let it be noted that the Bible does not ever explicitly condemn slavery. Yet, every precept in the Bible and everything we know about the God who gave us the Bible tells us that slavery is reprehensible to God. We ought not to ignore that people calling themselves Christian have practiced slavery. True, but the historical fact is that it was a purely Christian movement that led to the abolition of slavery, first in England, then in France, and finally in the United States, and ultimately across the entire world. Would polytheism, naturalism, or pantheism ever have produced the moral justification to end slavery? The simple answer is no.

Christian theism proposes that human beings are all made in the image of God. It gives the most significant dignity to human beings of all the worldviews we have considered. Does materialism tell us that "All men are created equal and are endowed by their Creator with certain unalienable rights?" This is an inherently Christian statement. It is not supported by empirical evidence. Neither is it well-supported by Islamic theism, dualism, or pantheism. The bottom line is this. Despite the many terrible things done by people who have called themselves Christians, the only worldview that could have produced the idea of human rights and women's rights is the Christian worldview.

Of course, our humanist friends will object. Our agnostic neighbors disagree. But it is true. Nearly every good thing that our modern, Western societies have enjoyed has come from biblical ideas. These include advances in modern science, our strong sense of social justice, political freedom, human rights, and women's rights. They were born out of Christian theism. This is a historical fact. Postmodernists and atheists have hijacked the ideas they value most from Christianity—from a culture, no matter how flawed, created by people holding to Christian values. These worldviews do not support the very things that those holding to them value. Again, we should not ignore that Christians and "Christian" cultures have much to answer for. Yet, people in those very same flawed cultures held to a Christian worldview and produced all of these treasured ideas.

This is not just an accident. Correctly observed Christianity gives every human being, no matter how well or poorly endowed physically, mentally, emotionally, or financially, incredible dignity and value. In Christian theism, every single person has infinite value—Christian theism demands of its followers absolute honesty and integrity. But we have already said that other worldviews have similar moral ideals. The power of Christianity lies in its inherent motivation, which provides power for individual believers to live up to their stated objectives.

The comments of second-century Roman philosopher and physician Galen illustrate this fact. In his writings, he noted of the early Christians, "their teaching of 'rewards and punishments in a future life' led to a lifestyle 'not inferior to that of genuine philosophers.' To Galen, this fact was especially notable in the disciples' 'restraint in cohabitation, self-control in matters of food and drink, the keen pursuit of [social] justice, and contempt of death.'"[58] The Greeks had their seven virtues, but they believed that only a philosopher who dedicated his entire life to achieving these virtues could approach the Greek ideal. Yet, Galen noticed that the lowly Christians lived like "genuine philosophers." He also noted the source of their power. It was their "contempt of death." We know where this lack of fear of death came from.

Galen was not the only Roman pagan to notice the sacrificial lifestyle of the early Christians. Julian, "the apostate," son of Constantine, tried to return the Roman empire to its pagan roots. However, Julian was frustrated in his efforts by the impeccable lifestyle of the Christians. He said, "Atheism has been specially advanced through the loving service rendered to strangers and through their care for the burial of the dead. It is a scandal that there is not a single Jew who is a beggar and that the godless Galileans care not only for their own poor but for ours as well, while those who belong to us look in vain for the help that we should render them."[59] In this quote, "Atheism" refers to the Christians, who were called atheists because of their stubborn determination to worship only one God and not to do homage to the Roman gods.

The early church treated slaves and masters, men and women, Greek and barbarian as equals. They purchased the freedom of mine workers and took abandoned children into their homes. The first modern hospitals were converted churches. This explains the explosive growth of the early Church. It also illustrates that Christian theism, properly lived out, produces better people.

---

58 Richard R. Walzer, *Galen on Jews and Christians* (Oxford, UK: Oxford University Press, 1949), p. 10-16.

59 Edward J. Chinnock, *A Few Notes on Julian and a Translation of His Public Letters* (London: David Nutt, 1901) pp. 75-78 as quoted in D. Brendan Nagle and Stanley M. Burstein, *The Ancient World: Readings in Social and Cultural History* (Englewood Cliffs, NJ: Prentice Hall, 1995) pp. 314-315.

On the problem of suffering, we have seen why cultures dominated by materialists and pantheists have fallen short in meeting the needs of the destitute. We also noted that Muslims generally do a better job but, unlike the disciples of Jesus noted above, do little, if anything, for non-Muslims. Christians recognize that suffering, in and of itself, is not evil, but the Christian response to suffering is compassion for those who suffer. Arguably, the most incredible compassion ministry in human history is that of Jesus of Nazareth. *"Jesus went through all the town and villages... healing every disease and sickness. When he saw the crowds, he had compassion on them, because they were harassed and helpless, like sheep without a shepherd."* (Matthew 9:35-36) *"Religion that God our Father accepts as pure and faultless is this: to look after orphans and widows in their distress, and to keep oneself from being polluted by the world."* Can anyone argue with the claim that, of all the worldviews in the world today, the Christian who follows the example of their Messiah, Jesus, will be the best possible person? There is no close rival.

Our proposed list of qualities that make for a better person is that they are humble, generous, courageous, diligent, self-controlled, honest, self-sacrificing, compassionate, and peace-loving. The first eight of these qualities have already been covered. Let us talk about the quality of being a lover of peace. Christian theists follow a man who was known as the Prince of Peace, and for good reason. Jesus said to his followers, *"Blessed are the peacemakers, for they shall be called children of God."* (Matthew 5:8). In the same sermon, Jesus told his followers to love their enemies. This is the highest possible calling. It is not easy to put into practice. The quality of being a lover of peace is not just a commandment of Christ; it is also supported by the value and dignity of each individual, which is a foundational belief of Christian theism. Christian theism, consistently followed, produces the best possible human beings.

Calvinism: Deterministic Christian Theism

A significant aspect of the argument above that Christianity is true, right and better is based on the assumption that the Christian worldview includes the robust free will of every human being. Free will is supported throughout the Bible. This is exhibited with Cain, to whom God said, *"Why are you angry? Why is your face downcast? If you do what is right, will you not be accepted? But if you do not do what is right, sin is crouching at your door."* God also appealed to the free will of the Jews. *"This day I call the heavens and the earth as witnesses against you that I have set before you life and death, blessings and curses. Now choose life, so that you and your children may live..."* (Deuteronomy 30:19-20) Free will is also a basic working assumption in the New Testament. *"This is good and pleases God our Savior, who wants all people to be saved and to come to a knowledge of the truth."* (1 Timothy 2:4). God wants all to be saved, but not all are saved because many choose to reject the offer. It is worth bearing in mind that God's will is not always done, which is why Jesus prayed that it would be done in Matthew 6:10. This is not because God is not sovereign but because, in his sovereignty, God chooses to give free will to his children.

This foundational truth that God has given people the freedom to choose their path supports our explanation of why evil exists in a world created very good by an omnipotent and omniscient God. Free will is the basis for our understanding that God is love. It explains why we were made in the first place. Yet, a significant branch of the Christian world has either denied the existence of genuine free will before conversion or has significantly downplayed the Christian teaching of freedom of the will. This began with Augustine of Hippo (354-430 AD). It was carried into Reformed Theology by Ulrich Zwingli (1484-1531) and, most notably, by John Calvin (1509-1564). Augustine taught that before people are converted, they are totally depraved and unable to respond to the love of God. Augustine said, "Man's free will avails nothing except to do evil."[60] He taught what has been called double predestination—that God predestines both those who will be saved and those who will be judged and will go to hell. Julian of Eclanum, Augustine's contemporary, accused him of making

John Calvin (1509-1564)

God the author of both evil and good. He accused Augustine of taking his cues not from Jesus but from Manes, the founder of Manichaeism.[61] This accusation is not without merit. If Augustine were right (and he was not),

---

60 Augustine, On Free Will.
61 Augustine, *Contra Secundum Juliani Responionem Opus Imperfectum*, III.170.

then this would be problematic for Christian theism.

Ulrich Zwingli was the originator of what became known as Reformed Theology. He said, "God's sovereignty is the first principle of Christian thought... it is the hub that holds everything together."[62] Like Augustine and Muhammad, he raised God's sovereignty to greater importance than his love. Regarding salvation and damnation, Zwingli said, "Those individuals who end up damned forever in hell are also eternally determined by God for that fate."[63]

The theological system we are describing as deterministic Christianity is generally known as Calvinism. Therefore, we should consider what John Calvin said about free will, total depravity, and original sin. To Calvin, God's sovereignty trumps his love: "God is said to have ordained from eternity those whom he wills to embrace in love, and those upon whom he wills to vent his wrath."[64] In case there is any doubt about how Calvin believed this affected salvation, he also said, "For all are not created in equal condition; eternal life is foreordained for some, eternal damnation for others."[65] Regarding free will, Calvin said, "Even though we grant that God's image was not totally annihilated and destroyed in him (i.e., Adam), yet it was so corrupted that whatever remains is a frightful deformity."[66]

Calvin's deterministic theology has been summarized by the acronym TULIP, which stands for Total depravity, Unconditional election, Limited atonement, Irresistible grace, and Perseverance of the saints. Some modern Calvinists thoroughly embrace the five points of Calvinism. In contrast, others downplay Limited Atonement but cling tenaciously to the ideas of original sin, total depravity, and, especially, perseverance of the saints, also known as once saved, always saved. Many Christian evangelicals find their theological roots in Calvinism.

There are two critical points to be made about Calvinistic predestination. First is that it is not a correct biblical theology, and second is that, if it were true, then Christian theism would be significantly degraded as a "good" worldview.

---

62   Roger E. Olson, *The Story of Christian Theology* (Downer's Grove, Il: Intervarsity Press, 1999), p. 402.

63   Ulrich Zwingli, "On the Providence of God" in Jackson and Hinkle, *On Providence and Other Essays* (Durham, North Carolina: Labyrinth Press, 1983), p. 130.

64   John Calvin, *Institutes of the Christian Religion*, 3.24.16

65   John Calvin, *Institutes of the Christian Religion*, 3.21.5, as quoted in T. H. L. Parker, *John Calvin: A Biography* (London: John Knox Press, 2006), p. 142.6

66   John Calvin, *Institutes of the Christian Religion*, 1.15.4.

This book is not a study of biblical theology. For this reason, I will not give a thorough biblical refutation of Calvinistic predestination. Two good sources for this are *Life in the Son* by Robert Shank and *Troubling Questions for Calvinists* by F. LaGard Smith.[67] I will add two passages from the Christian Scriptures to those already used to support the correct view. *"He [Jesus Christ] is the atoning sacrifice for our sins, and not only for ours but also for the sins of the whole world."* (1 John 2:2). *"For the grace of God has appeared that offers salvation to all people."* (Titus 2:11) Christian determinism is not biblical. God loves his children equally and has made provision for all to be saved if they choose to do his will and accept his offer of a loving relationship with him. The Christian worldview includes a firm idea of human free will, which is the basis for God's love for humans and of humans for God.

This brings us to the second point. If the theological system known as Calvinism is true, then Christian theism is made to be significantly less good. It raises questions about whether Christianity is true, whether it is right, and whether it is better. Calvinism and Islamic theism have much in common. Both include a strong sense of fatalism and weak human free will if any. Both struggle to give a reasonable explanation of the cause of evil. Both worldviews propose that God is good but that God determines the ultimate fate of all of his creatures. If this is the case, God must be the author of both good and evil. If so, then the goodness of God comes into question. Is it true that God is good and also that God chooses to cause evil? These cannot both be true. Therefore, deterministic Christian theism, also known as Calvinism, falls short of the first of our qualities of a "good" worldview. With this logical inconsistency, it is difficult to defend deterministic Christian theism as completely true.

Is it right? Does a Calvinistic worldview produce satisfactory and reasonable answers to the questions people care about? Like Islamic theism, it does considerably better than most competitors but falls significantly short of the Christian worldview presented in this book. For example, on the question of our purpose, Christian theism says that we have a two-fold purpose: to give glory to God and to give and receive love from him. If Augustine, Zwingli, and Calvin are correct, then a large majority of humans

---

67   Robert Shank, *Life in the Son: A Study of the Doctrine of Perseverance* (Minneapolis: Bethany House, 1989).

were not created to give and receive love from God. Zwingli proposed that those who go to heaven and those who go to hell equally give glory to God. That is debatable. However, what is not debatable is that in the Calvinistic worldview, all are not equally valuable to God or loved by him. Both our value and our purpose are much degraded in deterministic theism.

Is it better? Does a fatalistic Christianity produce the best possible sort of human being? If everything that happens is according to God's sovereign will, surely this reduces the importance of our desire to do good. If people are mistreated, we might be tempted to say that this is God's will. If one particular nation or ethnic group is in a highly favored position over another, this may be God's will. The consistent Calvinist might even be comfortable with certain kinds of slavery. If God pre-chooses who will be saved, where is the strong motivation to help the lost to be saved? If those who are once saved are always saved, then the sense of urgency to continue to live a holy and productive life might be less. If deterministic Christian theism is true (which, thankfully, it is not), then one who consistently lives according to this worldview would not be the best possible person.

TWELVE

A Worldview Analysis of John 11

In the introduction, you were asked to consider how people of differing worldviews might view the scene in Bethany when Jesus raised Lazarus from the dead. There were two groups present at the resurrection scene. Their worldviews were similar, yet their slightly different worldviews produced very different interpretations of the empirical facts. This informs us of the power of worldview in determining how we interpret events and how we act in the world.

How would a materialist view the resurrection of Lazarus from the dead? The answer is that they would search for a "natural" explanation of what occurred. We can be sure they would look high and low for a non-supernatural explanation of what happened in Bethany. No matter our worldview, we all are highly reticent to interpret events in a way that violates our fundamental presuppositions. We can imagine a couple of possible explanations our atheist friend might devise to explain what happened when Lazarus came out of that cave. Our theoretical naturalist might propose that Lazarus was not dead. Maybe he had merely passed out before being placed in the tomb. After waiting patiently for four days, he strolled out of the cave when the stone was rolled away. The fact that Jesus said, "Lazarus, come out," at just that moment was merely a coincidence. Skeptics have proposed a similar explanation for the empty tomb of Jesus. Well, how then do we explain the foul odor? Maybe there was a dead animal in there with him. Hmmm...

Another possible explanation is that Lazarus had died and been laid in the tomb, but Jesus' disciples conspired to deceive potential followers. What they did was they found a person who looked much like Lazarus, wrapped him in grave clothes, moved the large stone in front of the grave the night before, and slipped the imposter into the cave. On cue, he walked out when Jesus called, "Lazarus, come out." Why a follower of Jesus would do such a thing is hard to say. It is worth noting that these explanations raise as many questions as they answer. The point is that we can be assured the materialist is very unlikely to change his or her worldview, but far more likely to produce a natural explanation, no matter how far-fetched.

Let us imagine a postmodernist in the crowd at Bethany. Forgive me if this sounds too much like a joke. A postmodernist walked into a bar... The postmodernist does not need to produce an alternative explanation of the facts. All explanations are equally true. Their main concern is to defend all witnesses' right to hold to their interpretation. The postmodernist likes to deconstruct metanarratives. Therefore, anyone using the resurrection of Lazarus to "prove" that Jesus is the Messiah and to disprove other explanations would receive a cold shoulder from our postmodern observer.

On the other hand, our theoretical postmodern attendee might be even more offended by the Jews who opposed Jesus. Our postmodern friend finds intolerance intolerable. Indeed, he or she would be horrified at the decision of the Jewish leaders to kill their opponent Jesus. The postmodern would likely prefer an explanation different, both from that of the disciples and of their Jewish opponents. But what would such an explanation be?

Also present in the scene is an animist or a polytheist. Theirs is a magical world in which supernatural events are commonplace. The apparent fact that Lazarus was raised from the dead does not upend their worldview. It does not cause them to want to kill Jesus. Neither does it inevitably lead them to declare him to be God-in-the-flesh. To them, Jesus might be a demigod, or the cave might be a local hot spot of spiritual energy. The raising of Lazarus was a marvelous experience for our animists or polytheist. He or she is nearly as overjoyed as Mary and Martha at the beautiful turn of events, but the miracle does not tempt them to move toward a monotheistic worldview.

And, of course, we have a guest in Bethany from the East. How will our pantheist visitor view the raising of Lazarus from the dead? The pantheist would envision Jesus as a guru—an enlightened one. It may even be possible to see him as an avatar—a personification of one of the Hindu gods such as Vishnu or Shiva. That Jesus would be a source of great wisdom comes as no surprise to our pantheist friend, but when he raises Lazarus from the dead, this will place Jesus in a particular category. Our pantheist friend might be more "open" to listening to what Jesus is teaching. Pantheists tend to have a more open, less doctrinal approach to spirituality. They would not resort to trying to kill Jesus. Who knows? Maybe our pantheist friend might even be open to hearing about Jesus as a savior. If so, they will have to change their understanding of God radically. The idea of God as a loving individual person, separate from the universe, will require a massive change of worldview for our pantheist visitor.

It would be a historical anachronism for us to imagine an Islamic theist in this scene. But let us suspend reality for a moment and put a Muslim at Bethany in AD 30. He or she is a theist, who believes in a personal God, but one who is quite distant and unapproachable. All was good for our Islamic theist until someone mentioned that just a few weeks ago, Jesus had said to a crowd, *"Before Abraham was born, I AM"* (John 8:58). The idea that God could come to the earth and dwell with people is a massive shock to a Muslim who sees Allah as too dignified to take on human form. He or she might accuse Jesus of the mortal sin of *shirk*—associating any human with God. Being a theist, there are two possibilities for our Muslim friend. Either he will join with the Jewish leaders in Jerusalem and aid in the plot to kill Jesus, or, like much of the crowd, he will see the incredible miracle as a sign from God and declare Jesus to be a prophet and perhaps the Messiah. Our Islamic theist, being a theist, will join one of the two factions created amongst the Jews that day. He will either make Jesus Lord or try to kill him.

THIRTEEN

Evangelism and the Christian Worldview

An in-depth comparative study of worldviews can greatly encourage those who began with the Christian faith. Hopefully, that has already happened for you. It is now time for us to think about how to put this newfound understanding of the superiority of the Christian worldview to use. How can we use our knowledge of the Christian and other worldviews to spread the gospel? Are there any examples in the Scripture to help us toward this end? Think about it. Jesus preached almost exclusively to monotheists. Peter and the other apostles did as well. Even Paul began with Jewish monotheists when he entered a new city. For many years I have used Peter's sermon in Acts two as a paradigmatic example of how to share the gospel with the lost. Here is my outline: 1. Tell them how Jesus fulfilled the Old Testament prophecy. Conclusion: Jesus is the Messiah. 2. Then tell them about Jesus as a miracle worker. Conclusion: Jesus is Lord. 3. Tell them about our responsibility for the death of Jesus. Conclusion: We need to repent. Tell them about the resurrection of Jesus. Conclusion: Let us be baptized into Christ to join in the death, burial, and resurrection of Christ.

At first, the outline above sounds like an excellent approach for our evangelism, and for some of our hearers, it may work well, but we need to consider the makeup of the audience in Jerusalem on the Day of Pentecost. One hundred percent of the hearers were monotheists who already understood the concept of moral absolutes and even of authoritative Scripture. In his sermon, there were many things that Peter could assume about his audience. There were many things that he did not need to explain to them. Fifty years ago, the situation in the United States and other Western nations was similar to that in Jerusalem in AD 30. Different for sure, but also similar. This is not the case anymore. The world has changed. We can take some cues from Peter's Pentecost sermon, but we may need to look elsewhere for a pattern of reaching those who do not hold to monotheistic presuppositions.

Fortunately, we do have one sermon in the book of Acts, which can be helpful for us as we think about how to evangelize those who hold to a worldview other than Christian theism. In most cities, Paul began by speaking to the Jews in their synagogue. Even in Philippi (Acts 16), where there was no synagogue, Paul found a place of prayer where God-fearers would meet. He was able to share the gospel with Lydia and others and to create an island of monotheists from which to plant the church there.

But when Paul arrived in Athens, the situation was completely different. Imagine him walking through the marketplace, looking for like-minded Athenians. He did find a small number of Jews and God-fearers, but for some reason, he made no headway with them. Instead, what he found was a city full of idols. It was a very religious city. The ordinary people were essentially followers of the ancient polytheistic Greek religions. The intellectual elite, of whom there were many in Athens, had disdain for the polytheism of the ordinary folks. They were attracted to the various schools of Greek philosophy, especially Epicureanism and Stoicism. Paul caught their attention. Perhaps this was because he came across as a very knowledgeable person. In any case, Paul was given the excellent opportunity to speak in the Areopagus. This is where the most highly educated and influential men of Athens gathered to discuss the various philosophies of the day.

What would Paul preach? One thing is for sure; he needed a different approach to bring Jesus Christ to people who had almost no exposure to the Jewish Scriptures and had a very different idea of God. Specifically, the Stoics had a worldview we would describe as deism, and the Epicureans were panentheists. Paul chose not to use the usual evidential apologetics he normally used with the Jews, in which he pointed out messianic prophecies and the miracles of Jesus. Instead, he had the brilliant idea of engaging his captive audience in a worldview argument. We will use his famous sermon in Athens as a model—as a paradigm for engaging our present post-Christian world with the gospel of Jesus Christ. Let us look at Paul's address to the Areopagus:

"People of Athens! I see that in every way, you are very religious. As I walked around and looked carefully at your objects of worship, I even found an altar with this inscription: TO AN UNKNOWN GOD. So you are ignorant of the very thing you worship—and this is what I am going to proclaim to you.

The God who made the world and everything in it is the Lord of heaven and earth and does not live in temples built by human hands. And he is not served by human hands, as if he needed anything. Rather, he himself gives everyone life and breath and everything else. From one man he made all the nations, that they should inhabit the whole earth; and he marked out their appointed times in history and the boundaries of their land. God did this so that they would seek him and perhaps reach out for him and find him, though he is not far from any one of us. 'For in him we live and move and have our being.' As some of your own poets have said, 'We are his offspring.'

Therefore, since we are God's offspring, we should not think that the divine being is like gold or silver or stone—an image made by human design and skill. In the past God overlooked such ignorance, but now he commands all people everywhere to repent. For he has set a day when he will judge the world with justice by the man he has appointed. He has given proof of this to everyone by raising him from the dead." (Acts 17:22-31).

Here is an outline of Paul's approach:[68]

1. Find common ground.

2. Give respect where respect is due.

3. Acknowledge the good. Do not attack—especially do not attack those they honor greatly.

4. Know and understand the worldview of your audience.

5. Introduce them to the Christian worldview. Begin to help them see where the fundamental differences lie and why the Christian worldview is superior to their own.

In Paul's address to the Areopagus, he does not go on the attack, at least not at first. Instead, he begins what he hopes will be a discussion. His first move is to find common ground. He compliments the Athenians for

---

68   I am adapting an outline from my friend Dr. Robert Kurka.

being "very religious." Then he notes the foolishness of the dozens of gods, even noting that the Athenians covered their bases by having a shrine to an unknown god. "How foolish is that?" he might have said. In this case, the Stoics and Epicureans would undoubtedly have agreed with Paul that polytheism is not a valid worldview. They have common ground with him. Paul also points out that God does not live in human-built temples. At this point, the philosophers in the Areopagus are in complete agreement. They felt superior to ordinary people with their ancient polytheism, carried on in idol-filled temples.

Then Paul plays an interesting rhetorical trick. He uses the fact that the Athenians worshipped an unknown god as an opening to declare to them the existence of a God that they did not yet know—the God of the Jews. Having acknowledged their commitment to being religious and having found common ground in renouncing the polytheism of the common Athenians, Paul then explains to them why the God of the Jews and Christians is superior to their understanding of the supernatural. To them, God is distant and unknowable. To the Stoics, God does not involve himself in human affairs. We are all alone in the universe. To the Epicureans, God is an ineffable One and not a person.

The Greek polytheist believes that people exist to serve the gods. Paul points out that the reverse is true. It is he who gives us "breath and everything else." Every other religion has people reaching out to a distant and unknowable God. Paul tells his hearers that God is reaching out to us. He "marked out our appointed times and history." God has given each of us a personal mission. Individually, we have great value to Him. God is hoping that we will respond to his loving attention to our lives—that we will "reach out for him and find him." This is no distant, unknowable entity. To the panentheist Epicureans, God is part of creation. Paul tells his audience that God is not part of creation; he is the Creator who "gives everyone life and breath and everything else."

Next, Paul connects with his hearers by quoting their well-known authors. He quotes Epimenides, the Cretan philosopher, "For in him we live and move and have our being." It is as if Paul is saying, "See, what I am preaching to you is not as different as you think, yet YHWH is different, and he is better." Then he quotes the Stoic philosopher Aretas. "We are his offspring." The Christian idea is not as different as you think, but in every way it is superior. Paul sets an excellent example for us here. If we want to help bring a naturalist to faith in Christ, we need to understand what the naturalist believes. We should read their authors and, ideally, know their worldview better than they do. The same for helping Muslims, Hindus, or Buddhists come to believe in the one true God. This is a long-term goal, which will require much study. Christians ought to spend more time in their own Scriptures than in reading the Qur'an or the Vedas, but we ought to have the goal of knowing well the worldview of those with whom we hope to share our faith.

Paul finishes his sermon with an appeal for his hearers to turn to the God of Israel. Yet, he leaves them feeling respected and listened to, not shamed or demeaned. It is striking that he only mentions Jesus at the end of his sermon after having already established the superiority of the Christian idea of God. Jesus enters Paul's sermon at about the three-quarters point of his story, which is about when Jesus enters the story in the Bible as well. Even then, surprisingly, he does not actually mention the name of Jesus. Personally, I do not suggest this strategy, but it is interesting. Finally, he points out to them the central truth of the Christian faith. Jesus of Nazareth was raised from the dead. This is a God who goes beyond being involved in human affairs. The God of the Jews has given us sufficient evidence to turn to him. He is one who intervenes for our good.

Did Paul's worldview argument work with this highly skeptical audience and prove effective? *"Some of them sneered, but others said, 'We want to hear you again in this subject.'"* (Acts 17:32). Paul left them wanting to hear more and to continue the discussion. Even those who were not convinced found Paul to be a well-informed and engaging speaker. Some of his audience, including Dionysius, a member of the Areopagus, came to believe in Christ. Our use of worldview arguments will not convince all non-believers. Yet, those few genuinely looking for the truth will have their minds opened. At this point, our lives must agree with the faith we profess. Our worldview argument may open minds, but it is the beauty of a life that has been transformed to the likeness of Christ that will open hearts to the gospel. The worldview argument is not a panacea. It is not a silver bullet. However, in a post-Christian world, it is an essential ingredient in our efforts to win souls for Christ. We plant and we water, but God gives the increase. Let us resolve to sharpen our skills at explaining and defending the Christian worldview as we plant and water. And to God be the glory.

Nihilism, Existentialism, and Marxism

In chapter five I evaluated the naturalist/materialist worldview, concluding that it is not true, that it does not provide satisfactory answers to the questions that people really care about, and that it does not naturally tend to produce the best sort of human being. One of the observations I made along the way is that for many who describe themselves as atheists or agnostics, their worldview appears to be more about what they do not believe in, rather than what they believe in. It is my experience that for most people, knowing what we do not believe in is not enough to satisfy. We want to know, not only what we do not believe in, but also what we do believe in. Many, if not most materialists eventually move from not believing in anything toward some sort of belief in something. Despite their belief that there is no supernal power, and no ultimate purpose to life, they have sought to create a human-generated, human-focused kind of purpose. In the process, humans have created a few sub-categories which fall under the atheist umbrella.

In the appendix, we will briefly consider three options that materialists have chosen in order to give themselves a sense of purpose. Well, not exactly, because one of the sub-worldviews we will consider in this chapter, nihilism, states categorically that there is no purpose or meaning to life at all. This list is not comprehensive, but it does represent three logical poles that atheists have moved toward. They are nihilism, existentialism, and Marxism. The first, nihilism, is perhaps the most honest of the three. The nihilist accepts the logical implication of atheism. Life is meaningless. End of story. Stop the search. Do not even try. There is no goal. Let us eat, drink and be merry, for tomorrow we die. The individual cannot create meaning for themselves, and neither can the group. The second, the existentialist, finds meaning in the individual. The goal in life is to poke reality in the eye and create meaning for oneself. We look death in the face, and go out there and create for ourselves a purpose, and a passion, and we live life the best we can for ourselves. If others do not like it, that is their problem. The third, Marxism, is the logical opposite of existentialism in that it wholly denies the importance of individuals. Meaning is found in societies. The purpose of individual life, if there is one at all, is to create communal good, to create the most good for the most people—to raise the wealth of the average person. What is important is the average prosperity of society, and the goal is to suppress individual selfishness for the sake of the common good. We remove people from the top and the middle rungs of the ladder—the super-rich capitalist class and the bourgeoisie, and we give their wealth to the masses—the working class.

Nihilism

It is debatable that nihilism is a worldview. It is a bit more like an attitude toward life. A helpful definition is that of Nolen Gertz; "Nihilism as an 'ideology of nothing' would not mean that we adhere to a discernable system of beliefs about nothing, but rather that the beliefs we have, or think we have, are equivalent to nothing."[69] However, nihilism is the most logical conclusion for anyone who genuinely accepts that there is no supernal reality, and that the only things which are real are physical things. If only physical things are real, then beauty, art, ethics, justice, free will, and purpose are meaningless words. Almost by definition, if atheism is a correct view of reality, then there is no purpose or meaning to life. If we accept this logical conclusion, we are tempted to go down the rabbit hole known as nihilism. Much of nineteenth and twentieth century philosophy is an attempt to avoid going down this depressing rabbit hole. In particular, much of what Nietzsche did in his philosophy was to seek an alternative to nihilism. Nietzsche pointed out that, "The acting man's delusion about himself, his assumption that free will exists, is also a part of the calculating mechanism."[70] He did not succeed all that well in his attempts

68   Nolen Gertz, *Nihilism* (Cambridge, Massachusetts: MIT Press, 2019), p. 6.
70   Friedrich Nietzsche, *Human, All Too Human*. Taken from James Sire, *The Universe Next Door: A Basic Worldview Catalog* (Downer's Grove, Il: Intervarsity, 2020), p. 88.

to find an alternative to nihilism.

Few have been willing to publicly embrace nihilism. In Russia of the 1860-80s a group of nihilists sought to overthrow the czarist regime. Their methods were destruction. Their aim was to destroy the regime and the society over which it reigned, with the hope of building an anarchist society out of what remained. Metaphorically, they wanted to burn down the house. They opposed all accepted social norms and advocated the end of private property, marriage, and religion. After repeated attempts, they succeeded in assassinating Czar Alexander II on March 13, 1881. However, their nihilist campaign was soon ended, with the death or imprisonment of all its leaders. Russian author Dostoyevsky's novels included nihilist characters, as they were part of his Russian society. There is something self-contradictory about a nihilist giving his or her life for a cause, even if that cause is nihilism, which proposes that there are no causes worth dying for.

Modern-day nihilism is not characterized by such violent anti-social terrorists. The nihilist is the one who refuses to do anything in particular. They question the status quo, simply because it is the status quo, without offering an alternative status. He or she plays video games hours upon hours or watches sports incessantly without caring who wins, or shops for hours upon hours, not in order to be the best-dressed person, but to avoid the boredom of doing nothing. Jerry Seinfeld is famous for being a comedian/philosopher who carries the banner of nothing. In his first public appearance after giving up his career of making jokes about nothing, David Letterman asked Seinfeld what he had been doing. Seinfeld responded, "I'll tell you what I do: Nothing. Doing nothing is not as easy as it looks. You have to be careful. Because the idea of doing anything, which could easily lead to doing something, that would cut into your nothing, and that would force me to have to drop everything."[71]

When we ask a nihilist why they did something, either "good" or "bad," they will refuse to explain themselves. They do not have reasons, only actions. When I was a child, my mother once asked me why I had done something bad. I responded, "Because I wanted to." This non-answer is the typical answer of a nihilist. It drove my mother crazy, as she could not argue against such a non-reason. To the nihilist, an offensive joke is

---

71 Taken from Nolen Gertz, *Nihilism* (Cambridge, Massachusetts: MIT Press, 2019), p. 5.

just a turn of phrase, intended to produce laughter. "What's the big deal?" he or she asks. To the nihilist, sex is simply two bodies joined together to produce pleasure. No more and no less. We can see that nihilism is surprisingly prevalent in modern society. For many, but not all, the rejection of the Christian worldview has led to the rejection of meaning. It has created a generation of couch potatoes.

If nihilism is a correct view of the universe, and in particular of the human condition, then there is nothing to know. There is only an infinite chain of cause and effect. Every thought is gratuitous. Existence is absurdity. A human being is merely a very complicated machine which we do not fully understand.

A cultural example of nihilism is found in the book *The Hitchhikers Guide to the Galaxy,* by Douglas Adams. In this book four time-travelers move back and forth, both in space and time, through the universe, from the Big Bang to the culmination of time, looking for the meaning in life. In their search, they come across a race of super-intelligent beings who built a massive, planet-sized computer named Deep Thought. The purpose of this computer is to discover the meaning of life. After seven and one half million years of calculation, the supercomputer finally spits out the meaning of life. It is the number forty-two. Life is reduced to absolute absurdity. The novel is fun to read, but Adams' conclusion is nihilism, which is not a particularly fun idea.

Friedrich Nietzsche ended his life insane. This is where true nihilism carries us. Ernest Hemingway, another who tended toward nihilism, took his life. There is a revealing scene in Hemingway's *A Clean, Well-Lighted Place* which expresses the psychological angst of nihilism. The nihilist life is, symbolically, a clean, well-lit place:

> It was nothing that he knew too well. It was all a nothing and a man was nothing too. It was only that and light was all it needed and a certain cleanness and order. Some lived in it [ie. a nihilist reality] and never felt it, but he knew it all was nada y pues nada [nothing and then nothing] y nada y pues nada. Our nada who art in nada, nada be thy name, thy kingdom nada, thy will be nada in nada as it is in nada. Give us this nada our daily nada and nada us our nada as we nada our nadas and nada us not into nada but deliver us from nada; pues nada. Hail nothing full of nothing, nothing is with thee. He smiled and stood before a bar with a shining steam pressure coffee machine.

This, in essence, is nihilism. It is a clean, well-lighted place where nothing of consequence happens. No wonder that nearly all atheists seek meaning elsewhere, no matter how poorly supported by their worldview. And thus, we turn to existentialism.

Existentialism

The search to avoid the obvious implications of materialism probably began the day it was first embraced. As many times as we might tell ourselves that there is no meaning to life, and even if our worldview informs us that this is in fact true, every fiber of our God-given being screams out against this falsehood. Life is not meaningless! In the highly individualistic culture of Europe in the nineteenth and twentieth centuries, a logical place to search for meaning, in a world which does not naturally produce it, is in the individual. Existentialism, then, is the approach to life which seeks meaning through individual action in the world. We create meaning for ourselves. Existentialist author Albert Camus expressed this angst over nihilism; "A literature of despair is a contradiction in terms... In the darkest depths of our nihilism I have sought only for the means to transcend nihilism."[72] Camus found the means to transcend nihilism in existentialism.

Unlike nihilism and Marxism, which are inherently and unavoidably atheistic, existentialism is not necessarily aligned with an atheistic worldview. In fact, the first great figure in the modern existentialist movement was Danish theologian and philosopher Soren Kierkegaard (1813-1855), who was a sincere Christian theist and opponent of the dry, intellectualism of Danish Lutheranism in his day.

Soren Kierkegaard (1813-1855)

But first, let us consider the Greeks. By the first century, many Greek philosophers had moved beyond the esoteric, metaphysical philosophies of Pythagoras, Plato and Aristotle to the ethical philosophies of Stoicism

---

72 Taken from James W. Sire, *The Universe Next Door* (Downer's Grove, Il: Intervarsity, 2020), p. 107.

and Epicureanism. These philosophies, which were dominant at the time of Christ, focused on the ethical implications of life—on discovering the essence of a life which is well-lived. Theirs was more a personal notion of truth—of a truth which is lived out, rather than believed in.[73] That being the case, theirs was an early form of existentialism—a deistic (epicureanism) or a panentheist (stoicism) version of existentialism.

Returning to Kierkegaard, he is considered the first modern existentialist. He was a fideist. In other words, he believed Christian faith is not based on rational proof, but on a simple trust in the God of the Bible. He considered the decision for Christ to be a leap of faith. He wrote, "The thing is to find a truth which is true for me, to find the idea for which I can live and die."[74] Kierkegaard said concerning truth that "the objective uncertainty, held fast in an appropriation process of the most passionate inwardness is the truth, the highest truth available for an existing person." The personal truth that Kierkegaard chose by a leap of faith is Christianity.

Having pointed out that existentialism is not inherently a naturalist worldview, the fact is that in the twentieth century, nearly every important existentialist has been an atheist. This is true for historical reasons. The twin disasters of the two world wars, along with the devastating implications of the Holocaust caused many in the intelligentsia in Europe, who had already rejected Christian theism to turn away *en masse* from a cold, dead atheism/nihilism and turn instead to a self-affirming existentialism. This includes authors Franz Kafka, Albert Camus, Simone de Beauvoir, and, most importantly, Jean-Paul Sartre.

Jean-Paul Sartre (1905-1980)

The acknowledged guru of existentialism is the Paris-born, Jean-Paul Sartre (1905-1980). He succinctly summarized his philosophy with the famous statement that "Existence precedes essence." In other words, first we exist, but then we make ourselves who we are by our free choices about how we live. He also said that "If God does not exist, there is at least one being in whom existence precedes essence, a

---

73   Here I am paraphrasing Thomas R. Flynn, *Existentialism: A Very Short Introduction* (Oxford, UK: Oxford University Press, 2006), p. 1.
74   Soren Kierkegaard, *Journals* (August 1835).

being who exists before he can be defined by any concept, and... this being is man." Man "defines himself."[75] Sartre proposed that the "purpose" of life is for the individual to live well and to live ethically. Truth is more a matter of choice than discovery. Atheist existentialists, including Sartre, seem to ignore the fact that their own worldview logically precludes the reality of free will and of non-deterministic human choice.

Thomas Flynn provides a helpful summary of existentialist thinking which works well across the spectrum of modern atheistic existentialism.[76]

1. Existence precedes essence. You are what you make yourself to be.

2. Time is of the essence. Death makes us time-bound beings who must redeem the time.

3. Humanism. Existentialism is an individual, person-centered philosophy. Meaning is found in the pursuit of personal identity.

4. Freedom and responsibility. Existentialism stresses freedom, and therefore also personal responsibility for how we use our time and talent.

5. Ethical considerations are paramount. As atheists, existentialists reject absolute moral and ethical truth, but the examined life in pursuit of personal ethical "truth" is supreme.

The essence, then, of modern existentialism is the individualized pursuit of meaning, value and purpose in a world which seems to lack it. Existentialist philosophers such as Sartre, Camus and de Beauvoir embraced liberal causes and emphatically championed democracy. They devoted their lives to social and even moral reform (again, despite holding to the belief that there is no objective moral truth). Sartre said that "in every moral choice we form an image of the kind of person we want to be and, indeed, of what any moral person should be."[77] To Sartre, the goal of life is not to be "right," but to be authentic. To go with the flow

---

75 Jean-Paul Sartre, "Existentialism," reprinted in *A Casebook of Existentialism*, ed. William V. Spanos (New York: Thomas Y. Crowell, 1966), p. 289.

76 Thomas R. Flynn, *Existentialism* (Oxford, UK: Oxford University Press, 2006), p. 8.

77 Ibid, p. 46.

is to live unauthentically. To stand heroically against the flow, living by one's personal conviction is to live authentically. The greatest good in existentialism is to live authentically. Even if we do not accept the existentialist philosophy, we can admit that, on the face of it, this is a "good" way of looking at life—to stand up for what we believe in in the face of opposition. By the way, it is also the diametric opposite of the postmodern view, as postmoderns are very skeptical of the ethical hero.

If we choose materialism as our overarching worldview, surely existentialism is to be preferred to nihilism. The atheistic existentialist is committed to living an ethical lifestyle, even if his or her ethics is not supported by any essential truth about the universe. The existentialist has a sense of purpose and meaning, which is better than living a pointless existence. Traditionally, existentialists have exhibited lives committed to such pursuits as personal freedom, women's rights, caring for the needs of the poor and other socially-conscious human causes. Producing meaning by individual commitments and choices might seem selfish, and is some ways it is selfish, yet the lives of many existentialists show that this commitment to living a purposeful life may indeed lead to a life of personal sacrifice. In the end, however, existentialism in its subjectivity suffers from nearly all the worldview problems of materialism, as we will reflect below.

Marxism

As a person raised in a hyper-individualistic culture which embraces personal freedom as virtually a national religion, it is difficult for me to provide an unbiased description of Marxism. Yet, I will make the attempt. Historically, Marxism is a reaction against nihilism while, at the same time, moving in the diametric opposite direction of existentialism. In other words, Marxists hold unambiguously to a materialist worldview. However, they reject the logical implications of materialism, which is that life has no inherent value or purpose. In other words, they reject nihilism, but they also reject the existentialist idea that meaning and purpose is created by the individual. Instead, the Marxist view is that value is found in creating the greatest "good" for social groups, rather than for individuals. Under the influence of Karl Marx (1818-1883) and his close associate Friedrich Engels (1820-1895), the good which ought to be created by societies became economic wealth for the working class. Marxism is a political and economic philosophy which stresses that the human purpose is to raise the material/economic prospects of the mass of the working class, the proletariat, at the expense of the individualistic prospects of the wealthy capitalistic class which Marxists call the bourgeoisie. To the Marxist, value can only be validly measured as a statistical average of a group. Individuals have no inherent value in this system. This is a problem for Marxism.

As stated earlier, it is possible to be a theist and also an existentialist. However one cannot rationally hold to either nihil-

Karl Marx (1818-1883)

ism or Marxism and also be a theist. Marxism is atheist at its core. In fact, another label for Marxism/Leninism is dialectic materialism. This is the philosophical approach to reality which insists that the universe is inherently material and that matter precedes thought and action.

To understand Marxism one must understand the thought of its founder, Karl Marx. Marx was born into a solidly middle class and politically liberal German family. His grandfather was Jewish. His father converted to the Lutheran faith for practical reasons. He was not at all religious. Karl was schooled in the classic liberal dialectic philosophy of Georg Wilhelm Friedrich Hegel. In 1844 he met his lifelong associate Friedrich Engels in Paris. Together, they developed the economic philosophy which we know of as Marxism. The two agreed that the capitalist system which then controlled the economies of the West was inherently unstable and self-destructive. They also saw it as inherently regressive in that it created massive wealth for a very few and left the mass of humanity behind economically. We will have to admit that there is at least some truth in this premise.

Marx claimed that, over time, the greedy bourgeoisie would only increase in wealth, and that the proletariat would become progressively more impoverished. History has confirmed the first claim, but not the second prediction. Since the mid-nineteenth century there has been a significant increase in the prosperity of the working classes in Europe and North America (which partially explains why Marxism has not caught on there). Marx believed that the working class—the proletariat—would eventually rise and overthrow the capitalist bourgeoisie to create a new economic system. He predicted that the revolution would begin in the capitalist West, where there existed a large proletariat class. Ironically, the first successful Marxist revolution happened in 1917 in Russia, where there was only a tiny working class. The economic system he and Engels proposed is known as Marxism. The political system they proposed, which would enforce the new economics, we know as Communism. Marx's great written works are the *Communist Manifesto* (with Engels, 1848) and *Das Kapital* (1867).

The essence of Marxism is political and economic. Important terms are the proletariat, the bourgeoisie, productive labor, labor power, exchange value, surplus value, means of production and class struggle. In Marx' view, class divisions are the chief important social groupings. In order to maximize the economic good of the working class, Marx proposed that private property should be outlawed. The only way to take economic power from the greedy capitalists is through a proletarian dictatorship. This can only be achieved through revolution, and most likely through violent revolution.

Let us be reminded what we are talking about. If there is no God; if only material things are real, then what is the source of purpose, meaning and value? The Marxist answer is value is found in social groups, or to use Marxian terms, in the class struggle. As one Marxist has put it, "The manner in which any society organizes production and the productive relations which follow, determine the chief characteristics of that society."[78] Or, "the relation between two classes can be only one of struggle."[79] To Marx and Engels, history is the study of the struggle between the classes. Marxists assume that the means of production of useful goods ought to determine all other social phenomena, including legal, cultural, artistic and political systems. In the process, if a few individuals have all of their possessions appropriated by the dictatorship of the proletariat, then so be it, as the desires of the individual are immaterial to the good of the society, which is the only good. As Marx said in his *Communist Manifesto*, "Workers of the World Unite, You Have Nothing to Lose by Your Chains and a Whole World to Gain."[80] He also expressed his belief that social good

---

78 Philip Sharnoff, *Principles of Scientific Socialism: A Primer on Marxism-Leninism* (Palo Alto, California: Ramparts Press, 1983), p. 13.
79 Ibid, p. 128.

trumps individual interests in his famous statement, "From each according to his ability, to each according to his need."[81]

Of course, to Marx, religion, and especially the Christian religion is a friend to the monied classes (never mind that Jesus said in Luke 6:20, *"Blessed are you who are poor, for yours is the kingdom of heaven."*). He said that "religion is the opiate of the people." Marx did not hold back in his disdain for all cultural practices which he perceived as favoring the bourgeoisie over the workers and the farmers. To him, this definitely included all religious belief. To summarize, Marxism provides humans with a sense of purpose and meaning. This value is not found in the individual, but it is a quest to give the means of economic production to the underclasses, and, ultimately, to create a classless society in which all needs are met and no one is cut off from the general prosperity produced when all share equally in the work. Even if we do not accept the conclusion, it is not difficult to see why some, especially the oppressed, have found this to be an attractive idea.

True, Right, Better: Are Nihilism, Existentialism and Marxism Good Worldviews?

Because nihilism, atheistic existentialism and Marxism fall under the materialist umbrella, and because materialism was covered in chapter five, only a very brief analysis of these worldviews is necessary here.

Are they true? The answer in each case is a clear no for the same reason that any worldview which denies the reality of a Creator is proved false. Something exists, and the universe was, apparently, created, which means that there is a Creator. Besides, absolute moral truth is real. Therefore, these three worldviews are not true.

Are they right? Do they provide reasonable, consistent answers to the questions people care about? With nihilism, the answer to this question is obvious. Nihilists propose that there is no purpose, no meaning and no value to life. They deny the reality of objective moral truth. Nihilism flunks this question on all levels. Nihilism is at the very bottom of the worldview pile.

---

80 Karl Marx and Friedrich Engels, *The Communist Manifesto,* Gareth Jones, editor (London: Penguin Press, 2002).

81 Karl Marx, *Critique of the Gotha Program,* (1875), trans. Kevin B. Anderson and Karel Ludenhoff (PM Press, 2023)

Both materialist existentialism and Marxism are marginally better than nihilism on this question. The "purpose" of existentialism is to create purpose and meaning in universe which seems, to the atheist, to lack both. Put it this way, if one seeks value and meaning in life, existentialism offers something, and something is better than nothing. Even if we believe, philosophically, that there is no objective meaning to life, at least let us live a life in which we produce a kind of personal meaning and in which we live ethically. This will help us to avoid the feeling of desperation which naturally is produced by a meaningless life. It will give us motivation to use our available time and energy to make a difference in this world.

Marxism provides no clear value or meaning to the individual, but it does provide at least a sense of social, if not individual purpose. Even if we are merely a cog in a machine, at least that machine has a purpose, which is to create the greatest economic good to the greatest number of people. We can reasonably predict that for the oppressed in the world, this will improve their material lot. The fact is that many communists have an almost religious zeal for their cause, and surely to have some sort of a cause is better than to be stuck in the depressing downward spiral of nihilism.

Are they better? Let us not even bother with nihilism. That is too depressing a thought. Can we reasonably predict that the atheist existentialist will be humble, generous, courageous, diligent, self-controlled, honest, self-sacrificing, compassionate, and peace-loving? If we look at the lives of some of the famous existentialists, we can see the qualities of courage, diligence, self-control and even generosity in order to pursue lives of personal purpose. Existentialists love heroes and existentialism has produced some heroes. This is superior to postmodernism. It is vastly superior to nihilism! However, in the end, existentialism is an individual-focused worldview. That it will produce self-sacrifice, committed honesty and compassion is a dubious proposition at best.

And as for Marxism, it barely manages to improve on nihilism. Marxism does not recognize the significance or dignity of the individual. It gives precedent to the statistical average person rather than to the actual autonomous human being. Unlike nihilism which (thankfully) has never become an accepted idea in any culture, and existentialism which also has not formed the foundation for any government, the Marxist experiment has been tried. Marxist or formerly Marxist states include the Soviet Union, Maoist China, the Pol Pot regime in Cambodia, Cuba under the Castros and North Korea. The result of these experiments speak for themselves. From almost any possible perspective these experiments were utter failures. They may provide a note of self-sacrifice, but words such as diligent, generous, compassionate, and peace-loving do not come to mind. Communists counter-argue that these attempts failed because they were incomplete. We can be thankful that they remained incomplete.

www.ingramcontent.com/pod-product-compliance
Lightning Source LLC
Chambersburg PA
CBHW021642120626
46545CB00002B/663